SpringerBriefs on Cyber Security Systems and Networks

Editor-in-Chief

Yang Xiang, Digital Research & Innovation Capability, Swinburne University of Technology, Hawthorn, Melbourne, VIC, Australia

Series editors

Liqun Chen, University of Surrey, Guildford, UK
Kim-Kwang Raymond Choo, Department of Information Systems and Cyber Security, University of Texas at San Antonio, San Antonio, TX, USA
Sherman S. M. Chow, Department of Information Engineering, The Chinese University of Hong Kong, Hong Kong, Hong Kong
Robert H. Deng, School of Information Systems, Singapore Management University, Singapore, Singapore
Dieter Gollmann, Hamburg University of Technology, Hamburg, Germany
Javier Lopez, University of Malaga, Malaga, Spain
Kui Ren, University at Buffalo, Buffalo, NY, USA
Jianying Zhou, Singapore University of Technology and Design, Singapore, Singapore

The series aims to develop and disseminate an understanding of innovations, paradigms, techniques, and technologies in the contexts of cyber security systems and networks related research and studies. It publishes thorough and cohesive overviews of state-of-the-art topics in cyber security, as well as sophisticated techniques, original research presentations and in-depth case studies in cyber systems and networks. The series also provides a single point of coverage of advanced and timely emerging topics as well as a forum for core concepts that may not have reached a level of maturity to warrant a comprehensive textbook. It addresses security, privacy, availability, and dependability issues for cyber systems and networks, and welcomes emerging technologies, such as artificial intelligence, cloud computing, cyber physical systems, and big data analytics related to cyber security research. The mainly focuses on the following research topics:

Fundamentals and Theories

- Cryptography for cyber security
- Theories of cyber security
- Provable security

Cyber Systems and Networks

- Cyber systems Security
- Network security
- Security services
- Social networks security and privacy
- Cyber attacks and defense
- Data-driven cyber security
- Trusted computing and systems

Applications and Others

- Hardware and device security
- Cyber application security
- Human and social aspects of cyber security

More information about this series at http://www.springer.com/series/15797

Darren Quick · Kim-Kwang Raymond Choo

Big Digital Forensic Data

Volume 2: Quick Analysis for Evidence
and Intelligence

 Springer

Darren Quick
University of South Australia
Adelaide, SA, Australia

Kim-Kwang Raymond Choo
University of Texas at San Antonio
San Antonio, TX, USA

ISSN 2522-5561   ISSN 2522-557X   (electronic)
SpringerBriefs on Cyber Security Systems and Networks
ISBN 978-981-13-0262-6   ISBN 978-981-13-0263-3   (eBook)
https://doi.org/10.1007/978-981-13-0263-3

Library of Congress Control Number: 2018942006

Printed on acid-free paper

This Springer imprint is published by the registered company Springer Nature Singapore Pte Ltd.
part of Springer Nature
The registered company address is: 152 Beach Road, #21-01/04 Gateway East, Singapore 189721,
Singapore

Preface

In Volume 1 (ISBN 978-981-10-7762-3), the issues facing the practice of digital forensic analysis were outlined, highlighting the growing volume of data as a major issue to be addressed. This has occurred due to the continuing development of storage technology, consumer devices, and cloud storage, which has subsequently led to increasing backlogs of electronic evidence awaiting analysis, often many months to years, affecting even the largest digital forensic laboratories. In Volume 1, a method of reducing the volume of data for collection and analysis purposes was explored, resulting in a framework and process to reduce the volume of data for review and analysis to 0.206% of the original source data or media volume.

In this Volume, the focus is on the equally important aspects of analysis and presentation of digital forensic data, highlighting that the process is not just about collection and preservation, and it also includes analysis and presentation of digital and electronic evidence in a manner that is legally acceptable. Highly skilled and trained practitioners are best placed to undertake analysis, but the increasing volume of data gives an opportunity to explore and develop innovative methods to rapidly analyse a subset of seized data, thereby reducing the time a practitioner spends looking for those needles in ever-growing haystacks.

Using the intelligence gained during digital forensic analysis is another aspect explored in this Volume. The main focus of forensic practitioners is on attending to urgent and outstanding evidential analysis work, with little to no time to consider how other matters may provide valuable input to current investigations. For example, information stored on a phone seized for one investigation may provide information about an unrelated investigation. Without an intelligence or knowledge management process, this information remains unknown. Using data reduction, knowledge management, intelligence analysis, and data mining principles, a capability for faster searches for information to assist in a wide range of investigations may be possible.

The overall research process involved collecting and assembling a corpus of test data from a range of devices: mobile phones, portable storage, and computers, as well as other sources of digital forensic data. A process of data reduction was developed and used to reduce the volume of relevant data to enable timely analysis.

In this Volume, a process to enable rapid review and analysis is explored, which includes semi-automated information and entity extraction, link charting and link analysis.

The full forensic images and data subsets produced in the research in Volume 1 are used to explore processes of quick analysis and semi-automated information and entity extraction, including a process of value-adding to the data subset with open-source information, with positive results. The analysis process is applied to the test data corpus and real-world data to ensure the process is valid and applicable to real-world data and investigations.

The Digital Forensic Data Reduction and Data Mining Framework outlined in Volume 1 provides forensic practitioners with a methodology to guide through the process of digital forensic analysis, allowing for instances where the practitioner can decide whether to undertake full analysis or rapidly review a data subset of relevant data, which enables a much faster process of analysis. The framework has been designed that should the reduction and review process not discover evidence or intelligence of value, the ability to traverse to traditional full forensic analysis is built in. This is not seen in other digital forensic frameworks.

The Digital Forensic Quick Analysis methodology outlined in this Volume, outlines a method for practitioners to work through the process of analysis, and can be applied to DRbSI data subsets, or full forensic images, and serves to lay out a plan for practitioners to follow which encompasses a thorough analysis process. Current analysis methodologies, as published, focus on specific tools or investigations typologies (drug, fraud, etc.). The quick analysis process seeks to provide a method for practitioners to follow which is not necessarily aligned to a specific tool or investigation focus and is applicable to a range of investigation typologies, using a variety of tools and techniques.

The process of open-source data fusion with digital forensic data holdings highlights the benefits of inclusion of external source data (such as those available via the Internet and other stored information holdings), also potential benefits related to the inclusion of closed source data holdings such as records of a government agency, and confidential source data, such as surveillance information or other classified information.

The contributions of Volume 2 are: (1) a method to quickly analyse digital forensic data for rapid review and triage, (2) a method to analyse digital forensic data holdings for evidence and intelligence, (3) a method to extract and store intelligence from digital forensic data, and (4) a method of combining external source data with information holdings to improve the analysis process and use digital forensic data to support intelligence-led policing.

Adelaide, Australia   Darren Quick
San Antonio, USA   Kim-Kwang Raymond Choo

Acknowledgements

The permission of Elsevier (Chaps. 2, 4, 5) and AIPIO (Chap. 3) to reprint the respective copyrighted material is acknowledged. The views and opinions expressed in this book are those of the authors alone and not the organizations with whom the authors have been associated or supported.

Contents

Abbreviations

$MFT	Windows Master File Table
ACPO	Association of Chief of Police Officers
AD1	AccessData Logical Evidence File
CSV	Comma-separated value
CTR	X-Ways Logical Image Container
DOCX	Windows document format
E01	Encase Physical Evidence Format
EXIF	Exchangeable image file format
EXT3/4	Linux extended file system
FAT	File Allocation Table
FTK	Forensic Toolkit
HD	Hard Drive
HFS/+	Apple Hierarchal File System
HTML	Hypertext Markup Language
ICT	Information and communication technology
IEF	Internet Evidence Finder
iOS	Apple iPhone operating system
IP	Internet protocol
ISO	International Organization for Standardization
IT	Information technology
JPG	Joint Picture Group
L01	Encase Logical Evidence Format
LT	Laptop
MD5	Message digest
NIJ	National Institute of Justice
NIST	National Institute of Standards and Technology
NTFS	New Technology File System
OS	Operating system
OSX	Apple operating system
PC	Personal computer

PDF	Portable Document Format
PLIST	Property list
PPTX	Microsoft PowerPoint format
RAM	Random access memory
RTF	Rich Text Format
SHA	Secure Hash Algorithms
UFED	Forensic Software from Cellebrite for mobile device analysis
URL	Uniform Resource Locator
USB	Universal Serial Bus
VM	Virtual machine
VMDK	Virtual machine disk
XLSX	Microsoft spreadsheet format
XRY	Forensic software from MSAB for mobile device analysis

Keywords

Big Data · Big Forensic Data · Computer Forensics · Criminal Intelligence
Data Mining · Data Reduction · Data Volume · Digital Evidence
Digital Forensic Analysis · Digital Forensics · Evidence Discovery
Forensic Challenges · Forensic Computer Analysis · Forensic Computing
Forensic Intelligence · Intelligence Analysis · Knowledge Management
Mobile Device Forensic Extracts · Open Source Intelligence · Quick Analysis
Selective Imaging

Chapter 1
Introduction

As outlined in Volume 1(ISBN 978-981-10-7762-3), the significant growth in the size of storage media, combined with the increasing popularity of digital devices, accompanied with a decrease in prices of devices and storage media, has contributed to a major issue affecting the timely process of justice. The ever growing volume of data seized for analysis has been raised as a major issue since 1999 (McKemmish 1999). Lengthy backlogs of work has been one result of this (Justice and UDo 2016; Parsonage 2009) which the growing size of devices contributes (Garfinkel 2010), often now consisting of many terabytes of data for each investigation.

As digital forensic data consists of large amounts of structured and unstructured data, a variety of file systems, operating systems, software, and user created data, spread across a variety of devices, the analysis of this data demands a unique method of analysis. Time constraints add to the pressure to undertake thorough analysis in a timely manner, and the wide skillset demanded of practitioners puts additional pressure on timely analysis, with time needed for research and training to maintain a wide knowledge base.

Brown et al. (2005) stated the challenge in digital forensics is locating relevant information in large datasets, analogous to finding 'needles in haystacks', or in some instances 'bits of needles in bits of haystacks'. Beebe and Clark (2005) stated that 'the sheer volume and "noisiness" of…data is absolutely overwhelming and incompatible with manual data analysis techniques'. The unique requirements that make the field of forensic analysis different from traditional pattern analysis included; data that is both related and unrelated, 'interesting' data may be low frequency rather than repetitive, data sources are large and can include multiple sources, differing data types, and that the cost of missing relevant data is large (Brown et al. 2005). Sheldon (2005) stated that due to the increasing capacity of storage devices and the increase in time to undertake analysis, it is 'not feasible to continue performing forensic analysis using the accepted approaches that we use today'.

© The Author(s), under exclusive license to Springer Nature Singapore Pte Ltd., part of Springer Nature 2018
D. Quick and K.-K. R. Choo, *Big Digital Forensic Data*, SpringerBriefs on Cyber Security Systems and Networks, https://doi.org/10.1007/978-981-13-0263-3_1

Existing forensic solutions have evolved from the first generation of processing and analysis methods, and are beginning to address scalability, but a challenge remains in processing larger and larger datasets and locating crucial evidence and intelligence in a timely manner. In this book, a method of thorough analysis of forensic data subsets is outlined in detail, and the reader is guided through examples of analysis using test data, and then how the process can be applied to real world data. The process is also applicable to full forensic images, and serves to ensure thorough analysis is undertaken on digital forensic data, in a timely manner. Many of the processes can be run concurrently, so practitioners are not waiting for software to finish processing, they're undertaking a review of the output of processes whilst other processes are running.

In the first Volume, the processes of Identification and Preservation were covered. In this Volume, the focus is on Analysis and Presentation of digital evidence, mindful of the need to be undertaken in a manner that is legally acceptable.

In Volume 1, Chap. 3 introduced the Digital Forensic Data Reduction and Data Mining Framework (reproduced here in Fig. 1.1), and then stepped through how this provides for a forensically sound collection of a subset of data, along with provision for a timely and faster analysis process using data subsets, and the inclusion of external sourced data to inform decision-making. In this Volume, the process of Quick Analysis (Step 6) and Digital Forensic Intelligence plus Open Source Intelligence (DFINT+OSINT, Step 7) is outlined. It is again re-iterated that the Framework is designed so that it does not impede the normal process of digital forensic analysis, and has provision to revert to full analysis should the need arise. The benefit of the processes of Data Reduction and Quick Analysis are that if evidence or intelligence is located, the information may be available to the investigator in a faster timeframe, the case may be able to be finalised, and move on to the next one waiting in the queue. The process of Quick Analysis is outlined in the next chapter, Chap. 2.

Another aspect of this book is a discussion regarding the use of intelligence from digital forensic data, and the use of intelligence with digital forensic examinations. 'Intelligence' is information which is processed in some form into knowledge which is designed for action (UNODC 2011). There is potentially a large benefit to law enforcement, investigative, and other agencies, where information from disparate investigations can provide information and intelligence to assist other current and future investigations. Historically, there has been little discussion about the use of intelligence and knowledge management practices in the digital forensic realm, which is discussed in Chap. 3.

looseness-1The literature review also highlighted the prevalence of mobile devices, and the wide range and availability of data storage. Research was undertaken in relation to a method to process the extracts from mobile devices, reduce the volume of data, and aggregate the data into common formats for faster analysis. Including this type of disparate data within an investigation highlights the scope of the differing types of data that practitioners must process and analyse in a typical investigation. A method to process this disparate data in a timely manner and provide context to other source data is explored in Chap. 4. The use of open source information is discussed

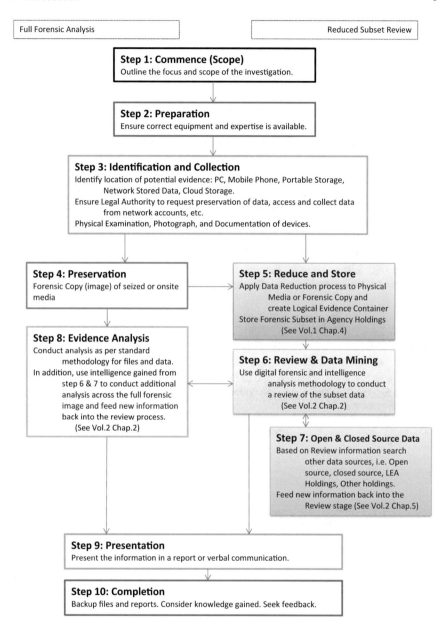

Fig. 1.1 Digital forensic data reduction and analysis framework

in Chap. 5, and the potential benefits to provide context to information located within digital forensic data and subsets.

The aim of this volume is to discuss the aspects of Analysis and Presentation, and the inclusion of external source data in the context of the Digital Forensic Framework. The aim of the overall process is to gain an understanding of the data seized in a timely manner, complying with legal requirements. This book outlines a process of rapid analysis, along with the use of open, closed, and confidential external source information, and benefits this can provide to evidence analysis, data mining and intelligence analysis. By applying data reduction and data mining techniques to atypical digital forensic data; i.e. large volume of structured and unstructured data, data reduction and intelligence analysis techniques are applied to test data and real world (anonymised) data to demonstrate the techniques can be applied in real world situations in an effort to address the digital forensic volume data issue.

In the following chapter, the Quick Analysis process is outlined, which addresses Step 6 and 8 of the framework. The process is outlined and experiments undertaken using the DRbSI data subsets, the test data corpus, and applying the process to real world data to demonstrate the application of the findings.

References

All URLs were last accessed (and correct) on 5 November 2016

Beebe, N., & Clark, J. (2005). Dealing with terabyte data sets in digital investigations. *Advances in Digital Forensics*, 3–16.

Brown, R., Pham, B., & de Vel, O. (2005). Design of a digital forensics image mining system. In *Knowledge-based intelligent information and engineering systems*, pp. 395–404.

Garfinkel, S. (2010). Digital forensics research: The next 10 years. *Digital Investigation, 7*, Supplement, no. 0, S64–S73.

Justice UDo (2016). *Office of the Inspector General. Audit of the Federal Bureau of Investigation's New Jersey Regional Computer Forensic Laboratory.* https://oig.justice.gov/reports/2016/a1611.pdf.

McKemmish, R. (1999). *What is forensic computing?*

Parsonage, H. (2009). Computer forensics case assessment and triage—Some ideas for discussion. Retrieved August 4, 2009, from http://computerforensics.parsonage.co.uk/triage/triage.htm.

Sheldon, A. (2005). The future of forensic computing. *Digital Investigation, 2*(1), 31–35.

UNODC 2011, *United Nations Office on Drugs and Crime—Criminal Intelligence Manual for Analysts*, United Nations, New York, Vienna, Austria.

Chapter 2
Quick Analysis of Digital Forensic Data

In Volume 1, the Digital Forensic Data Reduction Framework was outlined, which includes the process of data reduction; Data Reduction by Selective Imaging (DRbSI). The following chapter moves to the next stages of the framework (Fig. 1. 1) with a focus on Step 6 and Step 8, exploring processes of rapid or quick analysis of the DRbSI Data Subsets and Full Forensic Images.

In Volume 1, Chap. 4 it was outlined how data reduction can be applied to reduce collection and processing times, and provide investigators with evidence or actionable intelligence in a timely manner. The proposed Digital Forensic Data Reduction by Selective Imaging methodology, designed to reduce data volume and processing times, is a process of automatically filtering for key files and creating a subset of these files, and results in data subsets far smaller than the size of source media, approximately 0.206% of the source volume.

The aim of digital forensic analysis is to determine answers to investigation and enquiry questions; who, how, what, why, when, and where. Processing and analysis of full forensic images is undertaken to determine the evidential and intelligence value. This is achieved using analysis methods, such as that outlined in the EnCase Examiners Study Guide section 'Putting it all together' (Bunting 2012), the United States Department of Justice Digital Forensic Analysis Methodology (Carroll et al. 2007, 2008), and/or the United States National Institute of Justice Analysis Guidelines (NIJ 2004). Using an analysis framework in conjunction with a subset of data has the potential to identify information contained within electronic evidence faster than when compared with waiting to fully image and process entire media holdings for analysis.

In this chapter, the proposed Digital Forensic Quick Analysis methodology is detailed, which provides for review and analysis of information contained within digital forensic data subsets *and* full forensic images, including data obtained from heterogeneous distributed systems, in a timely manner. The Quick Forensic Analysis methodology is envisioned to provide for a thorough analysis of digital forensic data

Material presented in this chapter is based on the following publication:
Quick, D. and K.-K.R. Choo, Big Forensic Data Management in Heterogeneous Distributed Systems: Quick Analysis of Multimedia Forensic Data, Softw. Pract. Exper. 2016, https://doi.org/10.1002/spe.2429.

D. Quick and K.-K. R. Choo, *Big Digital Forensic Data*, SpringerBriefs on Cyber Security Systems and Networks, https://doi.org/10.1007/978-981-13-0263-3_2

and subsets in a rapid or timely manner, when compared with analysis of a full forensic image or extract.

The current process of digital forensic analysis is to create a full forensic image, process all the data, then review and analyse the data. Analysis is undertaken to ask specific questions about a case, including; who, when, where, what, why, and how. In criminal investigations and other enquiries, investigators will instruct a specialist regarding case information, and work in conjunction to answer questions and locate intelligence and evidence.

The United States (US) National Institute of Justice (NIJ) provide guidelines for forensic examination of digital evidence, which provides three examples of analysis methods; Timeline, Data Hiding, and Application and File Analysis (NIJ 2004).

The **Timeline analysis** process is described as a review of time and date information with a focus on data and log files relevant to an investigation.

The method for **Data Hiding** analysis describes the method of comparing file header information to a file extension to determine mismatched files (file signature analysis), and indicates practitioners should gain access to password protected files and compressed files.

The process for **Application and File Analysis** consists of a review of filenames for relevant files, examining file content, identifying operating systems, correlating files to applications, examining Internet history, examining unknown file types, default storage locations, user configuration settings, and file metadata.

The fourth section in NIJ (2004, p. 27) Ownership and Possession draws together a process of undertaking all three methods to place a subject at a computer, locate files of evidentiary value, and potential ownership identification. The NIJ methodology doesn't provide a method to undertake each process or analysis; rather it provides examples of the type of information to review and what to look for.

The United States Department of Justice (DOJ) Computer Crime and Intellectual Property Section (CCIPS) describe a Digital Forensic Analysis Methodology with a focus on analysis of files to answer questions relating to "Who/What, Where, When, and How" (Carroll et al. 2007). In addition; "Associated Artefacts and Metadata from Registry and Log files" are examined, along with "Other Connections", to "Identify any other information that is relevant to the forensic request". There is also mention of the "use [of] timeline and/or other methods to document findings". A range of general questions are listed as dot points under each section, such as; "Who or what application created, edited, modified, sent, received, or caused the file to be?" The CCIPS methodology doesn't specifically list methods or a process to undertake analysis; rather, it lists the questions a practitioner would endeavour to answer in relation to a file or data.

A method of analysis outlined by Bunting (2012) uses Guidance Software EnCase digital forensic software. This consists of a method of working through the processes available in Encase ranging from gathering case information, verifying file signatures, and examining Windows event log files. The method listed by Bunting summarises the various capabilities available in Encase software, and describes a methodology in a specific order for a practitioner to work through. The methodology is quite detailed, and designed around the use of EnCase software.

The methodologies outlined describe analysis using full forensic images of electronic evidence. An alternative process to rapidly understand digital forensic data is a process of digital forensic triage, with commercial forensic triage software now deployed in a wide range of agencies. The triage process usually consists of a scan of attached media, with a summarised report of findings according to what items were searched and reported on. Whilst this process can be quite efficient, the trade-off can be missing items of potential evidence or intelligence value. Better accuracy can be achieved, but this can considerably add to the search time. Another issue is that the output is usually a concise report, and the original files used to produce the reports are not always retained in a forensic container in native format. Whilst the triage solutions are deployed in a wide range of agencies to address the need for a rapid understanding of data, there remains a need to be able to collect specific original source data in its native format, such as in a logical forensic container, which allows for faster processing with a variety of tools, and presentation in court proceedings at a later date. Any source data subset collection process should also collect data in a timely manner.

The DRbSI digital forensic data reduction method outlined in Volume 1 enables the collection of a subset of data in a rapid manner, storing the data in a logical container, retaining source data and metadata (Volume 1 Chap. 4). The process uses common forensic software such as EnCase or X-Ways to access source media via a write-blocking mechanism, or loading a full forensic image into forensic software. Filters are used to identify and select pre-identified files and data that may contain relevant information. A process of thumbnailing video files, and reducing the dimension of picture files is available as an option to further reduce the data volume and collection time. The selected files and thumbnails are exported to a logical forensic container, and a full file listing is exported to spreadsheet. The next section outlines a methodology to conduct analysis in a timely manner by reviewing the data subsets which is then compared with processing and reviewing full forensic images.

2.1 Digital Forensic Quick Analysis Methodology

Analysis and review is undertaken to answer the general questions of an enquiry, such as; who, how, what, why, where, and when. This can include questions such as; who was using a computer or device at a particular time, what was being done, what websites were being visited, emails sent or received, documents written, spreadsheets or PowerPoint presentations produced, or when video files were played on a device. The scope of analysis can vary widely, and at the same time draw on similar file sources and data across a range of case types. There are often similar processes to be performed and related information to be gained, such as processing registry files for operating system installation details and user account information. Defining the scope of a request enables a practitioner to focus an enquiry, and should include general questions to answer, evidence or intelligence to be located, and what type of data will lead to an understanding of the case at hand.

Analysis can also answer important questions about where a person or suspect was, for example, locating pictures of a person on holiday can be of intelligence or evidential value to a case. Locating a C.V. or résumé of a person can also answer specific investigation questions. Examining the type of web searches undertaken can contribute to building a psychological profile of a user, and in some jurisdictions be of evidential importance (Fewster 2015). The analysis process can potentially locate evidence of specific offending, or evidence in relation to crime, such as organised crime activity or terrorism recruiting. By examining a range of file types; pictures, videos, documents, spreadsheets, emails, internet chat, website history, and other files, questions relating to investigations and intelligence probes can be answered.

Expanding out data from specific file types can further locate and add to information holdings. Data can be stored in a variety of source files, such as; Windows Registry files, Link files, Prefetch, Internet History, Apple plist files, Master File Table records, thumbcache files, etc. Couple this with the scope of an examination request, details of the device seizure, whether there is a suspected use of cloud services to commit crime, and other information, a digital forensic specialist can include the available information into a timeline of activity to explain users behaviour, and answer case specific questions. In addition, keyword searching can uncover further items of relevance, using crime or specific terms in relation to topics of interest, such as drug investigations, fraud, terrorism, organised crime, hacking, etc.

The overall process of analysis can be daunting, with a wide range of options available. A logical progression allows a specialist to ensure they have covered potential areas of enquiry, and examined many data sources for information. Without a framework in place, haphazard analysis can potentially miss key information. As an example, if a process is not run at the correct point, data may be missed or interpreted incorrectly, such as the incorrect interpretation of time and dates of Internet access resulting in incorrect conclusions being made (Boyd and Forster 2004). Hence, there is a need for a methodology for digital forensic specialists to follow to ensure an analysis process is sound, similar information is gathered from each device, and that processes are not duplicated.

Contemporaneous accurate notes of an examination are crucial to enable repeatability of processes to verify findings (ACPO 2006; NIJ 2004). This should include dates, times, actions and results observed. Information should be noted during analysis to enable specialists to verify the process used to analyse data subsets is repeatable and undertaken in a consistent manner.

The Digital Forensic Quick Analysis methodology is based on the processes described by Bunting and Wei (2006), NIJ (2004), and Carroll et al. (2007). It has been adapted and expanded to include additional processes and software, and is not software specific so the process can be undertaken using a range of digital forensic software. When software is mentioned it is as a guide to what is currently available to achieve a task, and forensic specialists are encouraged to use a variety of software to verify findings. The Digital Forensic Quick Analysis methodology is outlined in Fig. 2.1.

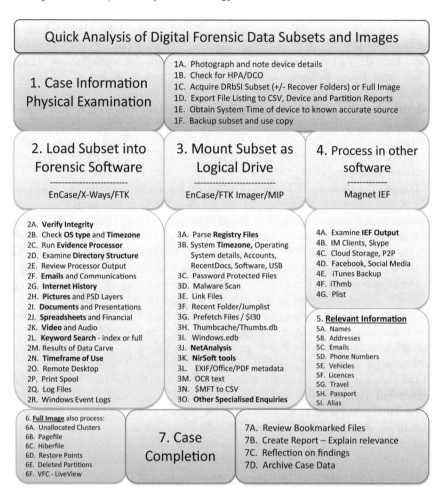

Fig. 2.1 Quick analysis of digital forensic data subsets and images—Steps 6 and 8 of the framework

2.1.1 Physical Examination

The first stage of digital forensic analysis is the physical examination of a device (see Phase 1 in Fig. 2.1). The information gathered at this stage may be relevant during analysis; hence, information about the physical device should be recorded, including; hard drive or storage media type, make, model, serial number, size, and other details (see Phase 1A). Whilst this can be achieved using software, the use of handwritten notes serves to highlight a person processing the physical media has physically observed the device, and in some cases, serial numbers or IMEI numbers can be electronically altered, and differ from the physical markings.

Next, storage media is identified, connected through a write blocking mechanism, and checked for presence of Device Configuration Overlay (DCO) and/or Host Protected Area (HPA) (see Phase 1B). Usually a full bit-for-bit forensic copy is made at this point, but as discussed in Sect. 2.2, this can take many hours. The process of Digital Forensic Data Reduction (Vol. 1 Chap. 4) outlines a process of initially collecting a subset of data rather than a full forensic copy (see Phase 1C). Timely analysis of media will enable a specialist to determine what information is present in an appropriate timeframe, and the use of forensic data subsets enable analysis to be undertaken in a faster manner than if having to wait for a full bit-for-bit copy to complete, verify, and then process.

The process of Recover Folders is a scan of the media to locate file and folder information and index remnants, and can result in locating additional files, with a trade-off in the time taken to scan the entirety of media or forensic images. The Data Reduction methodology includes the option of running the Recover Folders process during the collection of the subset, and this process can be undertaken at the discretion of the specialist, and the results documented during the collection stage.

The Digital Forensic Data Reduction DRbSI methodology also includes making a full file listing, i.e. by using the EnCase 'Export' function to produce a listing of all files and data in a spreadsheet format (see Phase 1D). This full listing may have information of relevance to a specialist during a review, and hence should be retained with the data subset, and examined as required. In addition, device and partition reports should be produced and saved with the file listing.

The physical system time of the device should also be obtained when possible and verified with a known accurate time source, and documented during the physical examination (see Phase 1E). When complete, the data subset L01 files are usually quite small, and a backup should be made, with the review able to be undertaken on a copy of the subset (see Phase 1F). If necessary, the information collected during the physical examination along with case related information should be reviewed by the specialist prior to undertaking analysis to familiarise themselves with case details and the physical media source for the forensic image or data subset.

2.1.2   Quick Analysis

In the Digital Forensic Quick Analysis methodology (Fig. 2.1), Phases 2, 3 and 4 are run concurrently to speed up the process of analysis. As an example; whilst waiting for one process to complete, other processes can be initiated whilst other results are being reviewed. When it is possible to run processes concurrently, this can achieve faster analysis results by utilising various software and processes at the same time, utilising the multitasking capabilities of computers, rather than running one process at a time, and waiting for processes to complete before moving on to the next.

It is acknowledged that the methodology will often move between Phases 2, 3, and 4, with information gained in differing phases being correlated with information from other phases, and whilst a process is running in one phase, the results of a different process from a different phase can be reviewed. This is done to speed up the overall examination process, and ensure that if relevant information is to be found, it will be located faster than a methodology which describes running one process at a time, with a focus on completing each step before moving to the next. A process which did this would be potentially clearer to explain, but would result in a less timely analysis process. However, each phase will be described without jumping around too much, although there are instances when concurrent processes will be discussed. The description is quite lengthy as the process is very thorough, but in application can be undertaken quite rapidly, as outlined in Sect. 2.4 when applied to real world cases.

Beginning with Phase 2, the data subset or subsets are loaded into forensic software, and initially run a process to verify forensic container integrity to ensure the contents have not changed from when captured (see Phase 2A). As the subsets are often quite small in comparison with full forensic images, this verification process is usually quite fast to complete. If a full forensic image is to be verified, this will usually take many times longer.

Phase 3 consists of mounting a subset or forensic image as a logical drive to enable other software to access the data, such as RegRipper, Malware scanning, link file analysis, Netanalysis, and other tools. Software such as Encase, Mount Image Pro, or AccessData FTK Imager, provides the ability to mount subsets or images as a logical drive. Notes should be made regarding the software used to mount as a logical drive, and the drive letter the subset or image is mounted as. Whilst waiting for the verification process to finish (Phase 2A), the process of mounting a subset can be undertaken.

Phase 4 addresses the inclusion of other forensic tools which can be used to process the data in the subset or image without mounting the image. Software, such as Magnet Forensics IEF (Internet Evidence Finder), is an example of this. Phase 4 can also be started whilst waiting for other processes to complete.

Returning to Phase 2 whilst the other processes are running, in forensic software such as EnCase or X–Ways, expanding the folders in a tree structure to view subfolders allows a specialist to gain an overview of the structure of the media, with 'User' folders, Windows folders, and other such higher level folders indicating the presence of an operating system, and the type of data that may be stored (see Phase 2B). An important first step is to check the time zone offset when an operating system is present. This can be achieved by running inbuilt functions of forensic software to parse the data from system files, such as Windows Registry files. In EnCase 6 this would consist of running the Case Processor EnScript with the 'Windows Initialise Case' option. Alternatively, using the 'View File Structure' option on the Registry file; C:\Windows\System32\config\SYSTEM, and locating the registry key 'TimeZoneKeyName' will indicate the Time zone setting. Bearing in mind there may be more than one control set, and the information in the initialise case report can be reviewed to determine the current control set if this is the case.

An alternative method to locate the time zone is to process the registry files with another tool (Phase 3A). Software, such as RegRipper, can be used to process the Windows Registry files; SAM, SYSTEM, SOFTWARE, NTUSER.DAT, and output the results to text file. It is often prudent to process registry files in forensic software and other tools to verify the results. RegRipper can be used to process Registry files from a mounted volume of the data subset. RegRipper output can be reviewed for details of the time zone setting of the device (see Phase 3B). Whilst reviewing the RegRipper registry reports for the time zone information, operating system details can also be observed and noted, such as the installation date, registered owner, last shutdown, and other relevant information. The SAM report relates to user account information, and the SYSTEM and SOFTWARE reports will have a range of information, such as the connections of external storage devices via USB or shortcut information, network connections, recent documents, software details, and other system related information. Any information of relevance should be noted. The output files can be quite lengthy, but can be reviewed in a timely manner to determine information of value.

Returning to Phase 2, using the information regarding the time zone setting, the setting in the forensic software should be examined to ensure the correct offset is applied. As an example, if the time zone setting displays 'Pacific Standard Time' as the offset, it is important to ensure that the forensic software is applying this offset. A note should be made of the time zone setting, and a confirmation that the forensic software is using the correct offset for calculations, once this has been verified.

Next, Phase 2C consists of running a variety of processing options. In EnCase 6 this would consist of running 'Tools|Search' with a variety of options, and EnScripts, such as the 'Case Processor' EnScript. A variety of initial processing options can be run, such as; file signature analysis, hash analysis, expand compound files, and other available options. When running these processes over a subset, the processing time should be many times faster than when running over a full forensic image. As an example, 'Tools|Search' includes; Keyword searching, Hash value calculation, Email processing, Verify File Signature, Identify codepages, and Search for Internet History. The 'Case Processor' EnScript includes a variety of File Parsers, Information Finders, Case Initializers, and scanning options, although it is not recommended to run all options at once in the Case processor EnScript, with the practitioner selecting which are appropriate for a case at hand.

Whilst the processes in phase 2C are running, files and folders in user accounts can be reviewed, such as; the Desktop folder, Documents, Pictures, Videos, Favourites, Recent folders, Recycle Bin, and other such folders, for relevant information (see Phase 2D). Bookmarking and noting details and information gained from any files of relevance to an enquiry, such as; resume's, relevant pictures, link files indicating encryption or other obfuscation type software.

When the phase 2C processing is complete, the results can be examined and any information noted, such as; the number of files with a signature mismatch reported, the type and number of email entries, and Internet History entries (see Phase 2E). When reviewing the signature mismatch files, any files which appear to be intentionally modified and not a result of software or operating system activity should be noted.

If processed, hash analysis matches to known alert files should be of particular focus, and bookmarked and details noted. When reviewing email results, files with possibly relevant information should be bookmarked and noted (see Phase 2F). The Internet History information can also be output to a spreadsheet for further analysis, such as creating pivot-tables of website visits (Phase 2G).

Picture files can be viewed in a gallery type view of thumbnails, noting of the total number of pictures displayed (see Phase 2H). This count of pictures can be relevant in Court situations, particularly in child exploitation investigations where the possession of illegal material is investigated, as often the question can arise as to how many pictures in total were present or reviewed. Any relevant picture files observed in the quick scan should be bookmarked and details noted. An area of additional enquiry with picture files are files with layers within the file, such as Adobe Photoshop "*.PSD" files. These may potentially contain multiple layers, with additional picture information in layers not necessarily viewable in a thumbnail view. Any relevant picture files with layers should be bookmarked and noted. Data carving processes can produce additional files for review, and any relevant should be bookmarked and relevant details noted.

Documents and spreadsheets should be reviewed, and bookmarked and noted when relevant, also noting the total number present (see Phases 2I and 2J). File-names should also be reviewed, and the contents of any files of relevance examined, bookmarking and noting relevant files and information contained within files. Financial software files, such as MYOB or Quicken databases, should also be examined, usually necessitating the need to view the files using the native software.

Whilst reviewing files a specialist should pay attention for the use of remote desktop type software (see Phase 2O) and encryption, such as EFS, Truecrypt, or other obfuscation methods (see Phase 3C). Password protected files can be processed within forensic software, or exported to be processed in other forensic tools, such as Passware Kit Forensic.

A filter for video files can be run across the subset, and any relevant videos bookmarked and details noted (see Phase 2K). If video files were thumbnailed in the collection stage, a major time saving benefit is that the thumbnails are easily reviewed in forensic software using gallery-view options. Digital forensic software usually has to fully export out a video file before it is able to be viewed, which can be quite time consuming when examining high definition video files which can encompass many gigabytes of data and take considerable time to export before being viewable, and are often dismissed as irrelevant when viewed. When reviewing thumbnail snapshots, determining relevance of video files can be quite rapid, with relevant files and data bookmarked. A rapid scan of thumbnails can determine if a video file is potentially relevant, or is simply a non-relevant video recording. If a video thumbnail file is potentially relevant, it should be bookmarked and noted, and full video file retrieved from the source media. A scan for keywords of relevant files and filenames, such as "pthc" for 'pre-teen hard-core' in child exploitation material (CEM) investigations can also be run across video file names, and other filenames and content in the data subset.

By this stage, it is quite often likely there are emails, documents, resume's, or other information which assist in understanding the person or persons using the device, and this information should be noted, with details such as; name, address, phone, email, and travel including overseas locations (see Phases 5A–5I). Drivers Licence numbers, vehicle registration details, passport details, or other relevant information potentially located during analysis should be noted. Alias information may be apparent, and tattoos on persons in pictures may be relevant, and should be noted as necessary.

Keyword searches can be run, in conjunction with an index, to locate any immediate matches, and a full search for any terms of relevance to an investigation (see Phase 2L). Also, if a keyword index was undertaken, the index can be reviewed for any terms that stand out, such as terrorism, or organised crime related terms, or keywords relevant to a case. In addition, a generic list of keyword terms can be used to alert for any not necessarily known about an investigation, but may change the focus of an investigation. As an example; whilst investigating a fraud matter, there may be internet searches for child exploitation material unrelated to the fraud matter, but potentially of more immediate investigation priority, should there be any indication of this activity.

A process of viewing all files sorted according to time/date, allows a specialist to determine key dates and times of events, such as; when the user folder was created, the last created or modified time/date of the last file, which can indicate the timeframe of use of a device (see Phase 2N). It is possible for the last modified or last file created time to be after the last recorded shutdown time. This can occur when a device has been put in sleep mode, hibernate mode, or the power was disrupted prior to a proper shutdown. This information relating to device usage timeframe may be particularly relevant in an enquiry.

Thumbnail and Thumbcache files can contain thumbnails of pictures which may be of high importance (see Phase 3H). These can be viewed, either within forensic software, or using other tools, such as ThumbnailExpert. This can be important, particularly when combined with information available from the Windows.edb file (see Phase 3I). As highlighted by Quick et al. (2014), Walsh et al. (2002), it is possible to merge the information from different sources to gain a better understanding as a result. In addition, exporting the contents of the Windows.edb file to a spreadsheet and reviewing the output can locate other information potentially relevant to a case.

With the data subset or full forensic image mounted as a logical drive, anti-virus and malware analysis software can be used to scan the mounted device for the presence of malware, and details of any found noted (see Phase 3D). Link files can be reviewed with forensic software, or reports produced using other software, such as Simple File Parser, by scanning the mounted volume or loading the files into software (see Phase 3E). Data within the link files can include relevant filenames and indications of any external drives, such as USB memory storage or hard drives. The contents of Windows/Recent folder Jumplist files, including the automatic.destinations files, can also be processed using software, such as Nirsoft JumplistsView, and the output analysed for any relevant entries (see Phase 3F). Prefetch files from the mounted subset can also be processed and the results examined along with $I30 INDX files which can also be processed with Simple File Parser (see Phase 3G). Any relevant findings should be noted.

The results of the IEF scan, when completed, should be reviewed for relevant information, such as Instant Messaging Chat, Skype records, Facebook messages, peer to peer software, torrent files, and other entries, which can be cross-checked in the forensic software being used to examine the subset (see Phases 4A–4D). IEF also reports on iTunes backup data and this should be reviewed noting any relevant items (see Phase 4E). IEF also reports on cloud stored data which can be compared with common log files such as SyncDiagnostics.log, snapshot.db, or config.db, available within cloud storage folders (Quick et al. 2014). IEF can process and report on a wide range of information and this should all be reviewed and noted when relevant information is located.

Netanalysis is another tool that can be started and run across the mounted subset to produce a report of Internet History which may include information not present in other reports, such as an EnCase Internet History report and reports from IEF (see Phase 3J). MSAB XRY or Cellebrite UFED can be used to process any iTunes MobileSync Backup folders and the output reviewed, which can be quite considerable in some cases (see Phase 4E). In addition, iThmb Converter can be used to examine the contents of Apple Photo cache files (see Phase 4F), and Plist files can be examined with tools such as PListExplorer (see Phase 4G).

XnView or other software can be used to produce EXIF spreadsheet reports which may provide information linking devices, such as; the serial number of a digital camera or the geophysical location of a photograph (see Phase 3L). At this point other third party tools can be run across the mounted volume such as the suite of tools provided by Nirsoft; including; IEHistoryView, ExifDataView, SkypeLogView, Password tools, and other tools which may locate data relevant to a case (see Phase 3K). It is also possible to scan pictures and PDF documents and convert text in images to optical characters for indexing, such as with FreeOCR or SimpleOCR (see Phase 3M). This can be particularly useful with screenshots from mobile devices, which can include contact and communication which may not be stored as text. Other files, such as Microsoft Office documents, spreadsheets, and PDF files can contain important metadata which can be exported to spreadsheet format for analysis purposes (see Phase 3L).

Windows Event logs can be examined for any events of note, particularly looking for any indications of a user changing time settings (see Phase 2R). Other software tools, such as Event Log Explorer, may assist. The contents of an $MFT file can be exported to a spreadsheet using tools such as mft2csv for review and comparison with the information presented within the forensic software to verify what is being observed (see Phase 3N). Print spool remnants may also be present and should be reviewed, and any log files examined for relevant case related information.

Other specialised enquiries can be undertaken at this stage, depending on the scope of the case, or there may be sufficient information obtained to answer the questions of an investigator or interested person (see Phase 3O). If no information was located during analysis of a subset, this does not necessarily indicate there is nothing there, but should indicate the device may require analysis of a full forensic bit-for-bit copy of the device, and this should be undertaken before ruling out the device as not containing evidence or intelligence value (see Phase 6). The full analysis process may not necessarily need to duplicate the processes already undertaken on a subset and could initially focus on processing data not already processed in the subset, i.e.

unallocated clusters, hiberfil, or pagefile. This could also include searching other data remnants such as System Volume Restore Points, or scanning for deleted partitions (see Phases 6A–6E).

Another way of gaining insight into the use of a device is a process of using a full forensic image with software, such as LiveView or Virtual Forensic Computing, which boots the image as a computer within a virtualised environment, and enables a computer to be operated and viewed as a user would have, and run software as a user would have (see Phase 6F). If evidence or intelligence was located at any point of this extensive process, this should be reported as per standard practice and agency requirements (see Phases 7A and 7B). Utilising the Quick Analysis methodology with a data subset can enable much faster collection, processing, and analysis of digital forensic evidence, and provide important evidence and intelligence to investigators in a timely manner. The process s discussed is quite thorough and encompasses a wide range of data sources, which is collected in the subset. The information potentially available in the wide variety of data sources can often assist in forming opinions about; who was using a device, where a device was used, what was done, how data was accessed, when a device was used, and potentially build a psychological profile of a user to answer the questions about why something has occurred.

Important information can be located in folders such as; desktop, downloads, pictures, videos, my received files, and many others. The process is equally applicable to a variety of operating systems, such as; Windows, Apple, and Linux. Questions about the operating environment can be answered, and User account details, including timeframes of use. One of the final steps of the analysis process is to reflect on the case information, and as new sources of information are discovered, build these into standard collection and analysis processes (see Phase 7C). Once complete, files should be archived as per agency standard policy and procedure (see Phase 7D).

2.2 Quick Analysis of Test Data

In the following section, the application of the Digital Forensic Quick Analysis methodology is outlined using test data from the digital forensic corpus (Garfinkel et al. 2009). This serves to provide an overview of the process using a standard digital forensic image format. It should be noted that the forensic image files in the corpus are quite small in comparison with forensic images observed in real world cases. This can be explained in that the test cases are potentially designed to be quickly analysed in academic or classroom situations, and are not necessarily entirely reflective of real world usage over a period of years.

To provide an overview of the application of the Digital Forensic Quick Analysis method, the evidence file 'terry-2009-12-11-002.E01' (Garfinkel et al. 2009) was selected for processing. The 10 GB E01 file was opened in a new case in EnCase 7.10.05. Reviewing the details of the imaging process for the source hard drive revealed this to be forensically imaged from a 40 GB hard drive on 16/2/2011 at 09:10 AM. The time to capture the full image is not recorded in the report, and an estimate of 20 min is presumed, based on 4 h average for a 500 GB hard drive. The image file verified in 6 min 26 s, reporting no errors. A subset of data was collected into a logical LO1 container using the method of data reduction outlined in Chap. 5. This took 48 s, collecting 15,236 files, resulting in a 364 MB file. This information was noted, and the L01 file was opened in a new case file in EnCase 7.10.05.

The L01 data subset verified in six (6) seconds, with no errors reported. The file and folder system was viewed in the Encase 'tree pane' view, and a 'Windows' folder was observed. Access Data FTK Imager 3.4 was started and used to open the L01 image file, and mount the subset as a mapped drive. RegRipper 2.8 was used to process the registry files; SAM, SOFTWARE, SYSTEM, and NTUSER.DAT.

Information in the RegRipper SYSTEM report was non-conclusive regarding the time zone, so the SYSTEM registry file was viewed in EnCase, using the 'view file structure' option. Viewing the Time Zone Information key it was observed that the time zone set was "PacificStandardTime". The time zone for the evidence item was amended to Pacific Standard to reflect this, and noted.

Information in the SAM report indicates the Administrator account was used 8 times, and an account named 'terry' was used 24 times. The presence of the 'terry' account was confirmed when viewing the folder structure in EnCase, noting the creation date of "18/11/2009 17:05:21". In the RegRipper report, the last login recorded for user 'terry' was 11 December 2009 19:21:18 UTC, hence minus 8 h equates to 11:21:18 h. The 'terry' account is listed as a "Default Admin user" account, with a password hint of 'root'.

The SOFTWARE report shows that the device operating system is 'Windows Vista (TM) Business', and was installed on 19/11/2009 00:51:31 UTC, adjusted to 18/11/2009 16:51:31 h. The registered owner is listed as 'terry', and the organisation field is blank. The network type is listed as 'wired', and one USB portable device is listed, named 'Terrys Work', serial number '51491E64', connected to E: drive.

The SYSTEM report shows that the last shutdown reported as 11/12/2009 20:04:17 UTC, or 12:04:17 h PST. Viewing and sorting all files in EnCase by the creation date and last modified date, indicate this is accurate, with the last times recorded as 12:04:08 h. The RegRipper SYSTEM report lists the computer name is "M57-TERRY". Two USB devices are listed, a 'Lacie Rugged FW/USB' device with serial number '00D04B881007C255', and the USB device listed in the SOFT-WARE report, matching the serial number. The last network IP address assigned to the computer is 192.168.1.105, with the DHCP server on 192.168.1.1. The domain is named 'm57.biz'.

The RegRipper NTUSER.DAT report for user account 'terry' lists the following keylogging software of note:

- C:\Users\terry\Documents\Downloads**xpadvancedkeylogger.exe**
- C:\Program Files**XP Advanced Keylogger**\unins000.exe
- C:\Users\terry\Documents\Downloads\keylogger**FamilyKeyLogger-setup.exe**

AVG anti-virus is listed as being installed, as is 'CCleaner' software, and Mozilla Firefox web browser. The 'RecentDocs' and the MediaPlayer keys are empty, possibly due to the use of CCleaner. The shell locations for user folders indicate no changes to the standard locations, i.e. the standard path for video files is 'C:\Users\terry\Videos', pictures in 'Pictures', and Desktop in the standard location. The 'UserAssist' key shows link files for CCleaner, OpenOffice, RealVNC, Eraser, and Google Chrome, and the previously mentioned Keylogger software. This provides indications for what software remnants to look for, without ruling out other software or data, noting the presence of CCleaner and Eraser, which can delete and overwrite potential data of interest.

As highlighted, the information available within these registry files can provide a great deal of information, which may be of evidential or intelligence value. This information was obtained within a few minutes of review of the data subset, which itself was collected and verified in a matter of seconds.

After ensuring the time zone is accurate for the device, the evidence processor options in EnCase can be run. As this is processing a smaller subset of data, all options are selected to be run. When a full forensic image is processed, it is recommended to run processes in stages. Whilst this is processing, IEF 6.6 is started and all options selected for processing.

Whilst IEF and EnCase processor are running, the directory structure of the subset is examined in EnCase, with the following observations:

- The Desktop has business related files of potential relevance.
- The Documents folder has approximately 4,980 screenshots of a user Desktop with software and screensaver activity with the details; 'Pat McGoo, pat@m57.biz, Phone 831-555-1234'. Also located is a copy of a receipt from ABCTech for $300 for a 40 GB HDD dated 18/11/2009. Of note was a file located in the documents folder, which was the zip bomb file '42.zip'.
- A resume document file is located, with the Author metadata field listed as 'Terry Johnson'. A spreadsheet, PDF files, and HTML files of note are also observed, bookmarked, and notes made as to the contents. The HTML files observed relate to Keylogger results with links to screenshots, with time/date recorded and 'User: Pat' listed for each entry.
- In the Pictures folder, four pictures of computer equipment are noted and bookmarked.
- In the AppData\local\Microsoft\Windows Mail\ folder, 113 EML email files are located and reviewed. Numerous email messages are bookmarked, and the text and details noted where relevant.
- Located in the folder 'Contacts' under the terry user account are contact details for possible associates.

At this point, there is a considerable amount of intelligence and evidence which has been gained from the pictures, documents, contacts, and particularly the email files, including information relating to alleged sale of computer equipment. The email details of 'terry@m57.biz', and details of the persons communicating with this account can be used to build a relationship chart of persons 'terry' associated with, and the type of communications undertaken, such as that outlined in Fig. 2.2.

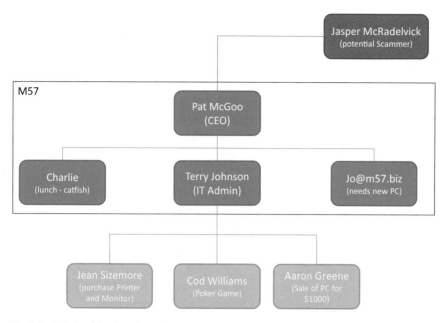

Fig. 2.2 Relationship chart for main entities in m57.biz Terry.E01 file

IEF completed in 2 min and 42 s, with results including Internet Explorer web history, Chrome, and Firefox web browsing history, parsed search queries, and browser Formhistory information, including email accounts; 'Russell.adam.m@gmail.com', and 't93940@gmail.com'. Details of this information is noted, along with; 'terry', 'm57', 'Dell computer for sale', 'CCleaner download' and VNC related links. The information in the IEF reports is exported to CSV format for further analysis.

There is enough information observed at this point to call a meeting with the investigator to discuss the evidence and intelligence located. If this is sufficient information to progress the investigation, a report can be produced from the bookmarked files, with additional information added to the report to explain the relevance of the files and data located. As the data subset is only 364 MB, this can be included with the bookmarked and exported files, and copied to a write-only CD. This satisfies the needs of preserving the information for further investigation, and Court purposes, and allows for additional analysis or processing if required at a later date. Whilst the E01 file in this case is only 10 GB, and could be split and copied to 3 × DVD's, in real world investigations, cases often comprise many terabytes of data which can be cost prohibitive to archive in their entirety, as long as the original source media is retained until investigation and Court proceedings are completed.

In addition, Encase processing of the subset completes in 16 min 9 s, with the following results:

- 88 compound files were located and expanded, nothing relevant was observed.

- 8278 Internet History Entries, which were exported to spreadsheet in CSV format for analysis. Also, 950 pictures were examined in a thumbnail gallery view, revealing most of the temporary internet pictures were previously observed in the picture gallery review, and nothing new or of relevance was observed.
- 2 email entries, in addition to the EML files already observed, but were not relevant.
- Windows Link files were processed, and 176 located, which included the previously noted 'VNC', Eraser and CCleaner entries.
- In the file signature analysis, 1096 files with incorrect header information were located, including picture files of potential relevance, which were bookmarked and noted.

If by this stage, nothing of relevance had been located, further processing of the data subset can be undertaken, including keyword searches on the names and details related to the investigation, scan for malware, examine jumplist files where present, process and review entries in Windows.edb files, matching information to thumbcache were possible. For example, if iTunes backup files are located, these can be processed with MSAB XRY or Cellebrite UFED software and the results analysed. iThmb files and plist files can be processed for information, and other tools can be used to process data, such as the Nirsoft suite of tools.

EXIF data can be extracted to spreadsheet for analysis, and OCR software used to process text in pictures and documents. Print spool files can sometimes include relevant information, and should be reviewed when present. If these enquiries result in limited relevant information being observed, analysis of a full forensic image would be the next step in the process, with a focus on the data not collected in the subset, such as unallocated clusters, pagefile, hiberfil, system restore points, other files and folders, and booting the forensic image using VFC or LiveView.

To undertake a comparison of the processing time for the data subset, processing the full forensic image in EnCase with the same options as undertaken on the data subset took 1 h and 24 min. No additional information was located in the full forensic image which had not been observed in the subset, i.e. the same emails were located, etc. Whilst additional Internet history entries were reported, many were duplicated information and the others were not relevant.

Processing the full forensic image in IEF took 47 min 53 s, and only minimal additional information were located, with nothing of relevance observed which had not already been located when processing the data subset. The EnCase 7 Case folder comprised 17.8 GB of data, in comparison with the data subset case file of 2.89 GB in volume.

In summary, collecting and verifying the data reduced subset took 54 s, with 2 min 24 s processing time for IEF, by which time the RegRipper reports were processed. Reviewing the data available after 3 min and 20 s revealed a considerable amount of relevant information, which was bookmarked and noted. In addition, a relationship chart showing linkages between entities was able to be quickly produced. Further processing of the data subset in EnCase took 16 min, but didn't assist in adding to the information already known.

This is in comparison with an estimate of 27 min for imaging and verifying the full forensic image, along with 48 min for processing in IEF, and 1 h and 24 min processing in EnCase, a potential total of 2 h and 39 min, in comparison with a total of 19 min for the Quick Analysis process.

Without including the EnCase processing times, it would be approximately 1 h 15 min for the full forensic image, in comparison with approximately 4 min for the subset collection and processing. As mentioned, this test example was a small hard drive, and in real world investigations hard drives are often in the multi-terabytes, which take considerably longer to fully image and process, compounded with multiple hard drives in devices, and multiple devices per case. In comparison, the data subset creation and processing times are minimal.

2.3 Quick Analysis of Real World Digital Forensic Subsets

To examine the application of the Quick Analysis process on real world data, historical case data from South Australia Police Electronic Crime Section (SAPOL ECS) was reviewed. All research was undertaken on site, and no data was removed from secure storage. The testing was undertaken using case data without completely viewing the contents, and minimal information was observed. The processing times and reported number of files was viewed and collated. Whilst this potentially limited full testing of the process, this was the appropriate method to undertake due to the confidential nature of the data. Testing was done on historical finalised cases.

2.3.1 Quick Analysis with EnCase on Real World Data

A case file was selected from historical archived cases, which included a data reduced subset collected when the case was finalised. The original source drive was a 500 GB laptop hard drive, which took 11 h to image and verify, resulting in a 387 GB E01 series of files. The subset was created using the Data Reduction by Selective Imaging process (Vol. 1 Chap. 4). This resulted in a 2.58 GB L01 file encompassing 10.6 GB of operating system files, user files, pictures, documents, emails, Internet history, and a range of other files. Video files representing 97.3 GB were thumbnailed at the time, and saved in a ZIP container of 44 MB.

The L01 subset was loaded into a new case file in EnCase 7.10.05, and took 2 min 54 s to verify (in comparison the E01 took 7 h to verify). The folder structure was examined, and User and Windows folders were observed. The Registry file "SYSTEM" was viewed, and a time zone of "Central Australian Standard Time" was noted. The subset was mounted as a drive letter using FTK Imager 3.4.1, and the directory structure was opened to the Windows/System32/Config folder to view the Registry files. RegRipper 2.02 was used to process the registry files; SAM, SOFTWARE, and SYSTEM.

The reports were opened and reviewed, with the following information noted in the reports:

- The username indicated the main user of the laptop, including a count of 295 logins. No other user account was present. The last login date was noted. The Administrator account only had 1 login recorded.
- The operating system was Windows 7 Ultimate, with the install date and the last shutdown dates noted, indicating a possible timeframe of usage of the laptop.
- Wireless network information was noted, including IP addresses allocated which indicate the use of two networks; i.e. one starting with '192', and another with '179' with a DHCP starting with '10'.
- USB Devices included an iPhone, an iPod, and 6 USB storage devices; Lexar, Sandisk, and Verbatim, with associated serial numbers, and dates/time information. This information could be correlated with USB and mobile devices seized at the time.
- The Skype service was noted (potentially relevant to a case where communications are involved).

The NTUSER.DAT file in the folder for the username observed in the reports was located, and processed in RegRipper, with the following observed:

- Skype shortcuts were noted, and games and applications shortcuts.
- The RecentDocs information included information relating to Pictures, Music, Videos, Documents, and ZIP/RAR files, many of which of potential relevance to an investigation.

The evidence processor options in EnCase were started, with the following options selected; Protected file, file signature analysis, hash calculation, expand compound files, Email parsing, and Internet history. Whilst this was running, Magnet Forensics IEF 6.7.0.0447 was started and the L01 processed with all options selected. Whilst these both run, the User folder was examined in EnCase, and folders including 'Desktop', 'Pictures', 'Video' and other locations were viewed, with the following noted.

- A resume for the user was located, providing relevant information such as, full name, address, phone numbers, work history, education, date of birth, and nationality.
- A total of 163,310 Picture files were present, many of potential relevance.
- Documents including saved Skype chat messaging were observed, and noted, providing relevant potential evidence.

The EnCase process completed in 1 min 7 s, with the following noted; 20,438 file signature mismatches, nil Email, and 7,117 Internet history entries. Relevant URL details were noted in the Internet History. IEF finished in 19 min and 59 s, and the following information was noted, and where necessary verified with the EnCase data:

- Encrypted PDF and DOCX files were noted.

- There were many thousands of items for review, including over 70,000 chat messages, Google search terms, web history, torrent information, and other information.

Two MobileSync folders were observed, and the files processed with XRY 6.15.0, with the following information.

- Located further chat messaging details of relevance.
- Also located Contacts, messages, pictures, and video files which may be of relevance to an investigation.

At this point as outlined there is a lot of intelligence and evidence of assistance to investigators. Further information may be available when processing link files, prefetch files, jumplists, and examining a variety of event logs and software log files. Software such as NetAnalysis could be used to verify the Internet history observed in EnCase and IEF.

At this stage the findings could be communicated to investigators, and a report prepared as required. If no information was located, or further enquiries are deemed necessary, keyword searches could be done, or a full forensic image could be examined, with a focus on additional data sources such as pagefile, hiberfil, and unallocated clusters.

As demonstrated, by undertaking a quick but thorough analysis process on a targeted subset of data, within a short amount of time a great deal of information can be located. Undertaking the same process on a full forensic image was tested, with the following times noted; 4 h for the full forensic image, and 7 h to verify, 5 h 15 min to process in EnCase, and 10 h 52 min to process in IEF, totalling approximately **27 h for imaging and processing**. In comparison it took 32 min to acquire the data subset, 2 min 54 s to verify, 1 min 7 s for processing in EnCase, and 19 min 59 s for IEF, totalling approximately **52 min**.

As outlined, there is a range of relevant information able to be located within 52 min, as opposed to 27 h for a full forensic image. In cases where timeliness is crucial, such as terrorism, child at risk, homicide, or other such cases, the additional 26 h could be crucial to progressing a case in a timely manner, potentially rescuing children from danger, or saving lives by identifying or locating a terrorism or murder suspect.

2.3.2 Processing with NUIX on Real World Data

NUIX is used also within SAPOL ECS as a review and analysis tool. The standard process is to create a full forensic image of exhibit media, and process this in NUIX with standardised options, depending on the investigation type. The test case available comprised of two laptop computers. To undertake a comparison, testing focused on three different methods; (1) a full forensic image of both laptop hard drives, (2) a Logical image of all entries observed in EnCase except unallocated clusters, pagefile,

Table 2.1 Forensic imaging volumes and times for SAPOL ECS data

		Time	Size (GB)	Compressed (GB)
1 LT HD	E01	10 h	750	380
	L01	2 h 6 m	103	69
	DRbSI	4 m	4.2	2.7
2 LT HD	E01	9 h	500	419
	L01	11 h 14 m	441	390
	DRbSI	12 m	8.6	3.98
Totals	E01	19 h	1250	799
	DRbSI	16 min	12.8	6.68
	Percentage	1.4%	1.02%	0.84%

and hiberfil, and (3) the Data Reduction process outlined in Vol. 1 Chap. 4 referred to as Data Reduction by Selective Imaging (DRbSI).

Using Access Data FTK Imager 3.2.0.0, full forensic images of the two laptops was completed, taking 19 h to image to E01, comprising 799 GB of compressed data volume from 750 and 500 GB source drives. Running concurrently this could be imaged in 10 h. Next, the hard drives were examined in EnCase 6.19.7, with all folders expanded in the table view and all entries selected except for; unallocated clusters, hiberfil.sys, and pagefile. A total of 103 GB of data was selected from laptop 1, and 441 GB selected from laptop 2. The selected files were copied to logical evidence (L01) containers, taking 13 h 20 min in total, or 11 h 14 min concurrently, resulting in 459 GB L01 files. Finally, the hard drives were again examined in EnCase 6.19.7, and the DRbSI process was used to filter for potentially relevant data, selecting the filtered files. The selected files were copied to logical L01 containers, taking 16 min in total, or 12 min concurrently. 12.8 GB of files were selected, which compressed to 6.68 GB in L01 files. Table 2.1 outlines this information.

NUIX 4.2.3 was then used to process the E01 and L01 files in separate cases, with the same options used each time. As outlined in Table 2.2, the processing time for the full forensic images (E01) was 5 h 43 min, resulting in a 14 GB case folder. The L01 logical images of all except unallocated was run for over 24 h but at this stage was only at 36%, with potentially two more days of processing required, therefore the process was stopped, as any process which takes longer than scanning the full forensic copy defeats the purpose of processing and analysing a subset of data. The Data Reduction subset logical images (DRbSI) fully processed in 34 min, resulting in a 3 GB case folder.

As can be seen in Table 2.2, there were more pictures in the subset (DRbSI) NUIX case (32920) in comparison with 32,275 pictures in the full image. This was due to the inclusion of 'Lost files' and deleted files which were selected when examined with EnCase 6.19.7 to create the DRbSI logical image. Additional processing with NUIX would potentially locate these extra files in the full forensic image, although this would further increase processing time of the full forensic image. Additional

Table 2.2   NUIX processing of SAPOL ECS data

	Time	Pictures	Documents	Emails	Folders size (GB)
E01	5 h 43 m	32275	598	285	14.3
L01	24 + h	Failed			
DRbSI	34 m	32920	506	287	3.05
Percentage	9.9%	102%	84.6%	100.7%	21.3%

emails were also located in the DRbSI NUIX case, although only two extra were observed. Fewer document files were reported in the subset, which is explained in that numerous licencing agreement files named 'licence.rtf' are excluded during the DRbSI process, although these can easily be included if deemed relevant, and would result in the same number of documents in both NUIX cases.

In this real world case, imaging and processing the full forensic images took a total of 24 h 43 min before being available for analysis. In comparison, the Data Reduction subset (DRbSI) collection and processing took 50 min and was ready for review. If the imaging was done concurrently, the full image and processing would encompass 15 h 43 min, and the DRbSI would be ready for review after 46 min, highlighting the timeliness of the data reduction subset process.

In a selection of twelve historical cases where an investigator had conducted a review of full forensic images and tagged items of relevance to an investigation, a comparison of the tagged files to the files in DRbSI data subsets highlighted that **all** the files selected as evidential in nature were present in the subsets. This supports that the data reduction process is valid in that the files in these cases were present in both the full forensic image and the data subsets, hence a review and analysis can be undertaken using a data subset in a much shorter timeframe and achieve similar results.

It should be noted that if evidential data was not located in review of a data subset, as will be the case in some investigations, analysis should then be undertaken on a full forensic image. The benefit of using a data reduction process is that relevant information may be located within a shorter space of time, such as 46 min in the test case outlined, compared with over 15 h to image and process the full forensic image, potentially alleviating the need for full imaging and analysis.

The Data Reduction and Quick Analysis methodologies have been observed to be faster than a process of fully imaging, processing, and conducting analysis. The data reduction process has also been of benefit when used in cases where full forensic images will not process in forensic software due to the volume of data, and also in instances of a hard drive errors and unable to complete a full forensic image. By using a targeted approach to collect relevant files, this enables collection of data sufficient to review for intelligence and evidence. In practice, it has also been possible to load many subsets into forensic software, which would potentially fail if using full forensic images.

2.4   Discussion

The process outlined for data reduction and quick analysis of data subsets has highlighted that data volume and processing and analysis time can be significantly reduced without a major trade off in information and accuracy. It is also acknowledged there are potentially cases which need full image processing and analysis, such as when evidence or intelligence information is located in unallocated space, pagefile, hiberfil, system volume restore points, and other locations not collected in a data reduction subset process. Whilst adding additional files to a subset will ensure this data is processed for analysis, in practice this resulted in longer subset collection time, larger container files for processing and archiving, negating the benefits of the data reduction method.

The examples outlined in the test data case from South Australia Police highlight that a great deal of information, intelligence, and evidence can be rapidly obtained from a quick analysis of a data subset, but should be reiterated that this process does not replace full analysis, and serves to provide a method to collect, process, and analyse data subsets in a timely manner to provide an understanding of where to focus investigations. The Quick Analysis methodology may alleviate the need for full analysis, where relevant evidence or intelligence is located during the review, and is deemed appropriate to satisfy the needs of an investigation or intelligence probe.

The methodology outlined gives digital forensic specialists a method and framework to review and analyse media in a timely manner. In many cases, this can focus investigations to specific devices which contain evidence or intelligence. Should a review be done and nothing be located, this does not mean the exhibit has nothing on it, but should then go through a full image and analysis process to determine if there actually is evidence or not. The Digital Forensic Quick Analysis methodology when used with forensic data subsets can be implemented as an alternative to triage processes, and the forensic subsets can be archived for any potential future enquiries, or re-processing as new methods are discovered. The process can also be utilised to examine digital media for actionable intelligence in a timely manner.

2.5   Summary

Data-centric approaches to ensuring the timely and efficient management of big forensic data due to the increasing data volume and the demand for service (resulting in large backlogs of cases awaiting analysis) are crucial. With the growing media volume, imaging and processing times are increasing. With the forecasted growth in heterogeneous distributed systems, this is estimated to continue to increase as companies meet the demand from consumers for more storage at cheaper cost. Forensic imaging, processing, and analysis times are growing; thus, identifying a need for a faster method to locate evidence and intelligence is critical. However, faster imaging and processing should not sacrifice accuracy. Many commercial triage methods utilise a scan of media, and report on an interpretation of data examined, but do not retain the source data in its original format.

The Digital Forensic Data Reduction process retains the original source data in industry standard format able to be read by multiple forensic tools. This also enables future processing as new methods are discovered. The Digital Forensic Quick Analysis methodology demonstrated that a rapid analysis of a subset of data can be achieved in a short space of time, and locate evidence and relevant intelligence. The application of the methodology to real world data highlighted the ability to rapidly collect and process a subset of data, consequently available for review in a timely manner.

The Quick Analysis methodology, combined with Digital Forensic Data Reduction, has potential to locate evidence and intelligence in a timely manner. With the back-log of cases growing ever larger, the process of digital forensic data reduction combined with quick analysis is offered as another tool available for digital forensic specialists, when timeliness of imaging and analysis is crucial. The next research opportunity exists to explore the ability to load multiple case subsets into forensic software to review and analyse entire case-holdings to determine if evidence or intelligence can be gleaned from cross case analysis using the proposed Data Reduction and Quick Analysis methodologies.

References

All URLs were last accessed (and correct) on 5 November 2016

ACPO (2006). *Good practice guidelines for computer based evidence v4.0*, Association of Chief Police Officers. Retrieved March 5, 2014, from www.7safe.com/electronic_evidence.

Boyd, C., & Forster, P. (2004). Time and date issues in forensic computing—A case study. *Digital Investigation, 1*(1), 18–23.

Bunting, S. (2012). *EnCase computer forensics—The official EnCE EnCase certified examiner study guide* (3rd ed.). Chichester: Wiley.

Bunting, S., & Wei, W. (2006). *EnCase computer forensics: The official EnCE: EnCase certified examiner study guide*. Indianapolis: Wiley.

Carroll, O., Brannon, S., & Song, T. (2007). *Digital forensic analysis methodology*. Retrieved September 19, 2007, from www.cybercrime.gov/forensics_gov/forensicschart.pdf.

Carroll, O., Brannon, S., & Song, T. (2008). Computer forensics: Digital forensic analysis methodology. *United States Attorneys' Bulletin: Computer Forensics, 56*(1), 65.

Garfinkel, S., Farrell, P., Roussev, V., & Dinolt, G. (2009). Bringing science to digital forensics with standardized forensic corpora. *Digital Investigation, 6,* S2–S11.

NIJ (2004) *Forensic examination of digital evidence: a guide for law enforcement.* http://nij.gov/nij/pubs-sum/199408.htm.

Fewster, S. (2015). Bernard Finnigan guilty: What the decision means for the law. *The Adelaide Advertiser.* http://www.adelaidenow.com.au/news/opinion/bernard-finnigan-guilty-what-the-decision-means-for-the-law/story-fni6unxq-1227603907259.

Quick, D., Martini, B., & Choo, K.-K. R. (2014a). *Cloud storage forensics*. Syngress: An Imprint of Elsevier.

Quick, D., Tassone, C., & Choo, K-K. R. (2014). Forensic analysis of windows thumbcache files. In *20th Americas conference on information systems* (*AMCIS 2014*), Association for Information Systems.

Walsh, S., Moss, D., Kliem, C., & Vintiner, G. (2002). The collation of forensic DNA case data into a multi-dimensional intelligence database. *Science and Justice, 42*(4), 205–214.

Chapter 3
Digital Forensic Data and Intelligence

This chapter examines the need for intelligence information in relation to digital forensic data holdings, and the potential to improve knowledge from a process of discovery. The need to undertake this in a timely manner is examined, including the potential for Digital Forensic Intelligence using a variety of disparate data, including DRbSI subsets, mobile device extracts, and other source data.

Terrorists, organised crime groups, and other criminals make substantial use of technology to aid their causes and commit crimes. The ability to silo their activities and maintain individual groups with minimal interconnections assists to hide their activities. The growth of technology, data volume, user storage, and connectivity, further assists to camouflage their activity. At the same time there is a growing volume of digital forensic data from computers and devices seized by enforcement agencies, resulting in a pool of potential intelligence information which may hold the key to uncovering organisations endeavouring to mask their activity.

The volume of data seized can be overwhelming, and present a barrier to intelligence analysis due to storage costs and processing time. A methodology which can reduce the volume of digital forensic data to enable timely search and review will assist with a process of gaining intelligence from the growing volume of digital forensic data. In Volume 1 a process of data reduction of digital forensic data has demonstrated an ability to reduce storage demands. This data reduction method enables the storage of extracts of many devices and computer data, and assists with indexing, searching, processing, and reviewing in a timely manner, as outlined in the preceding chapter.

Material presented in this chapter is based on the following publications:
Quick, D. and K.-K.R. Choo, Impacts of Increasing Volume of Digital Forensic Data: A Survey and Future Research Challenges. Digital Investigation, 2014. 11(4): pp. 273–294.
Quick, Darren. Digital forensic data and intelligence: Using data reduction to enable intelligence analysis. Journal of the Australian Institute of Professional Intelligence Officers, Vol. 23, No. 2, 2015: 18–26.

Organised crime groups and terrorist organisations are adept at splintering their activities, such that those in one group may be unaware by design of those in a neighbouring group, yet all working towards the same goal. These groups are highly skilled at separating their activities, and agencies entrusted with investigating these groups have a wider focus of review, skilled in stepping back to see a comprehensive picture, rather than focusing on individual cases. In our tremendously inter-connected world, with almost daily organised crime activity and terrorist incidents, there is a large amount of data residing on devices, computers, and mobile phones. Many of these are seized by enforcement and associated agencies, and yet often, the data remains siloed in case files and evidence rooms.

The interconnectedness of computers, combined with the Internet and mobile devices, has increased data volume and information well beyond what was once only imagined in science fiction. From our fingertips users can access current and global level knowledge bases once undreamt of. Combine this with cloud storage, pervasive computing, big data holdings, and vast stores of networked information, the information available to a user from a computer or mobile device is growing. The intelligence information available just from one individual device nowadays surpasses that which previously took many hours, days, or weeks to accumulate from a wider variety of sources.

By reviewing the information extracted from seized computers and mobile devices, the scope of a terrorist organisation or an organised crime group may be revealed. There is a large pool of data of potential intelligence value on these devices, with information which may link disparate entities through communications, associations, or other such records and files. There is a need to be able to examine the entirety of the data, which could reveal information linking current or cold-case crimes or prevent future crimes or terrorist attacks. The process of an encompassing review can be difficult with the growing volume of data, but there is a solution available to enable intelligence analysts to manage and review this growing digital information in a timely manner.

Currently, large volumes of device data is extracted and provided to investigating officers but rarely does this contribute to intelligence collection or analysis (Garfinkel 2006). This is perhaps due to two issues; (a) intelligence practitioners are not aware of the type of data on seized computers and devices, and (b) the volume of data makes it difficult to review, especially in a timely manner. Education and training can address the first issue, for example, interdepartmental collaboration between digital forensic specialists and intelligence personnel, along with specific education and training in each of the fields. Engaging digital forensic specialists in intelligence areas would enable agencies to fully realise the breadth and depth of digital information and its relevance to intelligence sections, in conjunction with the opportunity for collaborative engagement. In addition, providing access to digital forensic data to intelligence analysts with the appropriate specialised training to review and recognise the common factors in seemingly disparate information from various data holdings will enable the inclusion of digital forensic data to a range of intelligence probes. Successes in use of digital forensic data for intelligence will ultimately prove the worth of this data, and lead to a greater understanding of the potential breadth of uses, and positive outcomes, when inclusion of digital forensic data is considered.

The following discussion will outline how the Data Reduction by Selective Imaging process (Fig. 1.1 Step 5) as part of the Digital Forensic Data Reduction Framework has potential to assist not just forensic examiners, but intelligence practitioners as well. The DRbSI method to reduce the growing volume of digital forensic data is discussed in relation to a method to draw intelligence from this untapped pool of information.

3.1 Intelligence Analysis and Digital Intelligence

The discussion thus far has focussed on digital forensic data as evidence. However, there is a potential to utilise digital forensic data for intelligence and knowledge discovery, or 'digital forensic intelligence'. The Australian Crime Commission National Plan to Combat Cybercrime "acknowledges the need for a more accurate intelligence picture to assist in identifying emerging trends and better direct resources to areas which would have the most substantial impact on the activities of cyber criminals" (ACC 2013a). One method to achieve this is by gathering and analysing intelligence from electronic evidence held or seized by law enforcement agencies undertaking investigations. One difficulty preventing this is the "big digital forensic data" problem. The sheer volume of data causes issues in relation to collection, storage, analysis, archiving, and particularly, extracting and using intelligence from the seized data.

Evidence is data which is used to establish proof, whereas intelligence is information which is processed into knowledge designed for action (UNODC 2011). 'Criminal intelligence is the creation of an intelligence knowledge product that supports decision making in the areas of law enforcement, crime reduction, and crime prevention' (UNODC 2011). Intelligence-led policing is a model where crime intelligence and data analysis provide valuable input to a decision making framework in an effort to reduce, disrupt, and prevent crime through strategies and management (Ratcliffe 2007). A common misconception is that criminal intelligence is surveillance and other covert activities. However, a wide variety of information can be combined with covert information to provide a broader picture to be used by decision makers, and is then criminal intelligence (Ratcliffe 2007). There is a potential for digital forensic data to provide valuable information as part of the intelligence-led policing process, and criminal intelligence, which can also assist digital forensic examiners.

Three types of criminal intelligence are; Tactical, Operational, and Strategic (UNODC 2011). Tactical Intelligence supports front line staff and investigators, and is often tied to an investigation leading to an arrest or gathering evidence. Tactical intelligence is mainly short term, arrest-focussed activity directed to front line operational officers. Operational Intelligence sits at a broader organizational level to support area commanders and regional managers in crime reduction activity. This is a mid-level focus to assist with tackling organised crime groups, and for decision makers to determine the priorities for limited resource allocation. Strategic Intelligence aims to provide an understanding into patterns of criminal behaviour and the criminal environment, with a focus on future activities (Ratcliffe 2007). Strategic analysis is aimed at higher level decision makers, with a longer term focus (UNODC 2011).

The intelligence analysis process is a cycle of Tasking, Collection, Evaluation, Collation, Analysis, Inference Development, and Dissemination, visualised in Fig. 3.1 (UNODC 2011). As outlined in the Criminal Intelligence Manual for Analysts (UNODC 2011), the tasking phase is designed to outline the scope and requirements. The Collection phase is to identify and collect the data required to achieve the task. Data can be from open source, closed source, and classified information. Open source data includes information gathered from internet sources such as publicly available Facebook information, Twitter data, media reports, and Weblogs (blogs). Closed source data can include confidential internal reports and other information holdings. Classified information is data which a user must hold a suitable security clearance to access. The Evaluation phase is a process of assessing the source and quality of the information, often by rating information using a scale. Collation is the process of organising the data into a format to allow for retrieval and analysis. Data integration and analysis is a careful examination of the information to discover meaning. Various techniques are used, such as link charts, event charts, activity charts, financial profiling, and data correlation. Then the information is interpreted to determine relevance, and to develop inferences in relation to the key pieces of information. An inference can be as a hypothesis, prediction, estimation, or conclusion, and is then tested before acceptance. Dissemination is then the communication of the intelligence, as a formal report, formal oral briefing, weekly bulletin, or an ad hoc briefing (UNODC 2011).

The application of intelligence analysis techniques can potentially assist digital forensic examiners to process the vast information contained within common digital forensic investigations. Al-Zaidy et al. (2012) applied criminal network analysis techniques to text documents to discover direct and indirect relationships between persons, addresses, and other entities. Garfinkel (2010) discussed the process of 'cross-drive analysis', and stated that the perception of casting doubt on the admissibility of evidence has prevented the adoption of this technique. Cross drive analysis is the use of statistical techniques to correlate information within a single disk image and across multiple disk images, which has potential use for intelligence analysis.

Ribaux et al. (2006) discussed how traditional forensic case data can have valuable input to the crime intelligence analysis process, the benefits that can arise from this, and stated that forensic science should participate and provide input to crime intelligence holdings. Their discussion related to traditional forensic information, such as DNA, hair/fibre, blood, and ballistic analysis, and it is further argued that there is a lack of recognition of intelligence needs within the general forensic science community (Ribaux et al. 2010). There is also a great potential to utilise valuable information stored within the multitude of digital devices and data seized for digital forensic analysis, widening the scope of analysis to include criminal intelligence beyond only examining the data for evidential purposes. Weiser et al. (2006b) proposed a National Repository of Digital Forensic Intelligence, comprising four

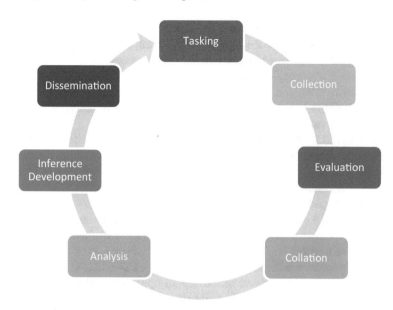

Fig. 3.1 The intelligence cycle (Adapted from UNODC 2011)

aspects; Information Knowledge Base, Best Practice, Tools Index, and a Case Index, with the aim of sharing ideas and methodologies leading to efficiency gains, however, impediments to large scale adoption of this included; control of data, confidentiality and classification, task load, and discovery issues. Initial establishment of such an intelligence capability is encouraged within and across agencies, as a first step towards a national data resource (see Australian Criminal Intelligence Database and Australian Law Enforcement Intelligence Network ACC 2013b).

Whilst Garfinkel (2010) raised the issue of lost opportunity for data correlation, it is discussed in relation to single investigations involving multiple drives, and the potential for examiners, who are working on one drive at a time, to miss data linkages across multiple drives. Whilst there is a great benefit to investigations to correlate data from multiple drives, there is also an opportunity to use stored subsets of data from a range of cases with intelligence analysis techniques to discover trends across a wide variety of investigations. This intelligence can also be used to provide management level information to determine the appropriate deployment of resources. There is potentially less hesitation to undertake cross-drive analysis if it can be communicated to examiners that forensic principles are not discarded, and traditional principles are observed to ensure the original media is not altered in any way. In addition, the use of data subsets facilitates the process of cross-drive analysis for many reasons, such as to research trends over time, gain tactical intelligence, and locate potential evidence. The data reduction process outlined in Vol. 1 Chap. 4 serves to collect a reduced subset of data for the purpose of a fast review, intelligence analysis, archiving, and undertaking future enquiries.

Raghavan et al. (2009) introduced the concept of an open Forensic Integration Architecture (FIA) to enable the merging of different evidence items and outlined a framework for formalising the analysis of evidence from multiple sources simultaneously. The FIA identified information from multiple sources to build theories relating to the investigation. However, the case study used demonstrated the concept applied for a single investigation, and was not discussed in terms of undertaking analysis across a variety of disparate investigations.

Alink et al. (2006) discussed the integration of mobile phone information into the XIRAF system to match information from other sources, such as forensic hard drive images. Case et al. (2008) proposed a framework and software termed 'Forensics Automated Correlation Engine' (FACE) which was intended to be an automated correlation of disparate evidence.

Garfinkel (2010) outlined a method of Forensic Feature Extraction (FFE), to be used to locate information within email communications, and potentially identify the primary user of a computer. This technique can be implemented across a variety of data subsets to locate intelligence in relation to communications across a variety of investigations, and can be utilised for tactical or operational intelligence purposes, along with other techniques applied to other data types.

Producing a profile of a suspect is another facet of criminal intelligence. Nykodym et al. (2005) discussed the application of psychological profiling techniques to create profiles in relation to cyber criminals and cyber-crimes. Abraham (2006) discussed the application of investigative or criminal profiling to identify the personality characteristics of a user, such as email authorship analysis. Shaw (2006) outlined the application of psychological profiling with insider threat cases using text analysis to identify suspects based on behaviour.

Garfinkel (2010) listed examples of areas to focus methods for representing and analysing information, which included signature metrics, metadata representation, system information, application profiles, communication information, and user profiles, based on what applications the user runs, when and why. Criminal profiling is potentially an intelligence process which can assist by having inclusion of digital forensic information, such as digital forensic data.

An opportunity exists to research methods of rapidly building a psychological profile of a user, based on the information observed within digital media. This could include information from seized media, such as; websites visited and times, Internet searches, Internet chat, information extracted from documents, spreadsheets and other user created files, the video files the user watches and stores, the music the user listens to, and other such information.

For a wide range of investigations, such as organised crime and terrorism related activity, there is a need to streamline the process of digital forensic collection and analysis, including preservation, review, analysis, and presentation. By improving the forensic collection and processing times, there may be an opportunity to include the gained knowledge with other information sources, such as news events (Xu et al. 2015a, b; 2016) to build a better picture of an incident or event.

There is also a potential benefit to a digital forensic examiner in liaising with investigators and reviewing intelligence holdings for a suspect or the user of computers and electronic devices. An examiner may be able to speed up analysis with prior knowledge of user, case, and investigation details, and provide more information to investigators, legal counsel, and other potential beneficiaries.

3.2 Digital Forensic Intelligence

Forensic Intelligence is; "the accurate, timely and useful product of logically processing (analysis of) forensic case data (information) for investigation and/or intelligence purposes" (Ribaux et al. 2006). This can be summarised as; knowledge from forensic data. Criminal intelligence analysis methodologies, such as those outlined in the United Nations Office on Drugs and Crime Criminal Intelligence Manual for Analysts, include link charts, timeline analysis, data correlation, and other analysis methods (UNODC 2011). By applying criminal intelligence analysis methodologies to digital forensic data extracts, there is a potential to gain a better understanding of computer and mobile phone data, and contribute to an increasing knowledge for tactical, operational, and strategic intelligence purposes.

There have been calls for a knowledge-base of digital forensic information (Harrison et al. 2002; Weiser et al. 2006a). One suggested model proposes a national repository of case findings to be stored with indexed scans of supplied data and a full text search system, in conjunction with text mining capabilities such as information extraction, topic tracking, summarization, clustering, concept linking, and question answering (Weiser et al. 2006a). At a national level this is an excellent goal to work towards, and within an agency a knowledge base could hold additional case related data, including the extracted data from mobile phones and devices, in addition to case findings provided to a national database. An Agency specific knowledge base could enable improved intelligence from extracted data.

Forensic intelligence and value adding to data can have a positive impact on case backlogs and improve analysis times, including in the field of Digital Forensic Services (van Asten 2014). It is shown by Ribaux and Margot (2003) that forensic data can improve investigation processes significantly. Forensic case data can contribute to intelligence analysis and provide areas for future investigation (Walsh et al. 2002). Analysis of forensic datasets can also contribute to cross-discipline and cross-offence typologies (Bell 2006). Furthermore, other intelligence analysis methods such as criminal profiling can assist when undertaking analysis of digital forensic data (Rogers 2003). A process of digital forensic intelligence analysis of mobile phone forensic data extracts can potentially result in accurate, timely, and useful analysis of a large volume of data extracts for a variety of cross-device and cross-case intelligence probes and evidential investigations.

Furthermore, secondary research highlighted a need to develop a framework, and procedures and guidelines for examiners to undertake in relation to intelligence analysis and the fusion of data from external sources. This highlights the need to build upon current methodologies, rather than create new frameworks to apply to investigations. The common digital forensic process of; identify, preserve, analyse, and present, is commonly used by examiners, however, some additional steps have been highlighted for inclusion, such as defining the scope of an investigation, and reviewing the results of an investigation.

Research also highlighted the trend in relation to the growing use of mobile devices, and the potential for evidence and intelligence to be stored within. To quantify this, a review of literature and case data was undertaken.

3.3   Mobile Phone and Portable Storage Growth 2003–2018

According to the ITU World Telecommunications ICT Indicators database, in 2014 the number of mobile phone subscriptions was near seven (7) billion (ITU 2014). At the time, more than 3.6 billion subscriptions were in the Asia-Pacific region, with 90% penetration in developing countries, and 121% in developed countries, i.e. more than one device per person (ITU 2014). In 2010 it was reported there was a steady growth in subscriptions from two (2) billion in 2005, to 5.3 billion in 2010 (ITU 2010). In 2014, the number of devices was reported to be growing, with more than one billion units shipped in 2013, up from 725 million in 2012, with 55% of the devices classified as smartphones (IDC 2014b). In 2013, smartphones and tablets outsold computers and laptops by four times (4X), up from one and a half times (1.5X) in 2011 (Bettini and Riboni 2015).

Popular operating systems for mobile devices include Apple iOS and Google Android. Research across 682,00 devices by Open Signal highlighted that there were 18,796 different Android device and version combinations in 2014, an increase from 11,868 in the previous year, and in 2012 there were only 3,997 distinct Android devices (OpenSignal 2014). This highlighted the growth in the variety of hardware and operating system implementations across Android devices.

The growth in the subscriptions and devices is coupled with the growth in storage volume of mobile phones. In the early 2000's, mobile phones had minimal storage, such as the Nokia 3310 model which mainly stored call and SMS information on the SIM card, whilst the RIM Blackberry 7230 had 16 megabytes (MB) of internal memory. In subsequent years, the volume of storage increased a thousand fold, with now (2016) popular devices including Apple iPhones of 128 GB and iPads of 256 GB. Memory card storage previously discussed in terms of 32, 64 and 128 MB, whereas in 2016, MicroSD cards are now discussed in relation to 32, 64 and 128 GB. Perhaps by the mid-2020's, MicroSD memory cards (if still used) will be discussed in terms of 32, 64 and 128 TB. Table 3.1 lists the growth in storage size from 2003 to 2015 of mobile phones and tablet devices; Apple iPhone and iPad, Samsung Galaxy, SanDisk MicroSD, and SD cards. This highlights that over the years, there has been a growth in storage available to consumers from 1 GB SD cards in 2003, to 512 GB in 2014 (see Table 3.1). Many Android and other devices have MicroSD memory card slots, which can further increase the storage volume available to a device.

Kryder's Law is the observation that hard disk storage density doubles every 12 months (Wiles et al. 2007). To assess the growth in portable storage, data relating

Table 3.1 2003–2018 size of popular mobile phone storage[a] (Information accurate 10 March 2018)

Year	Apple iPhone		Apple iPad		Samsung Galaxy		MicroSD	SD card	Price per GB
2003								1 GB	$330
2004								2 GB	$120
2005							512 MB		
2006							2 GB	4 GB	$55
2007	3 G	16 GB					8 GB	8 GB	$22.50
2008							16 GB	32 GB	$10.94
2009	3 GS	32 GB			i7500	8 GB			
2010	4	32 GB	iPad	64 GB	S	16 GB	32 GB	64 GB	$5.47
2011	4 S	64 GB	2	64 GB	S2	32 GB	64 GB	128 GB	$3.13
2012	5	64 GB	Retina	64 GB	S3	64 GB		256 GB	$3.52
2013	5 S	64 GB	Air	128 GB	S4	64 GB			
2014	6	128 GB	Air2	128 GB	S5	64 GB	128 GB	512 GB	$1.56
2015	6 S	128 GB	Pro	256 GB	S6	128 GB	200 GB		$1.99
2016	7	256 GB	Pro	256 GB	S7	128 GB	256 GB	1 TB	
2017	8	256 GB	Pro2	512 GB	S8	128 GB	400 GB		$0.62
2018	X	256 GB	12.9"	512 GB	S9	256 GB	512 GB		

[a]Compiled from http://apple-history.com/iphone, http://www.techradar.com/au/news/phone-and-communications/mobile-phones/the-samsung-galaxy-a-history-of-the-s-series-1227906, http://www.sandisk.com.au/about-sandisk/press-room/press-releases/, http://www.lexar.com/about/newsroom/press-releases

to the release date, storage volume, and price on release for SD cards from Lexar and Sandisk was collated (Lexar 2016; SanDisk 2016). The data is listed in Table 3.1 outlining the growth in SD cards from 2003 to 2018, showing that **SD cards have doubled in volume approximately every 15 months since 2003**. Based on the growth metrics from 2003 to 2014, the size of SD cards could reach 512 TB by the end of 2025. When examining the price per unit for SD cards on release, the price has decreased from $1.56 per MB in 2001 to $1.56 per GB in 2014, (based on the release price for the largest available SD card) and MicroSD cards are currently (2018) 62 cents per GB.

Along with the increase in the volume of storage data, there has been an increase in the software applications (or Apps) that users of mobile phones are using on the devices. The number of Apps available to users has increased since the introduction of App Stores, and in 2015 Android Apps totalled approximately 1.6 million, Apple's App Store had 1.5 million available, the Amazon Appstore had 400,000, and Windows Phone Store had 340,000 Apps available to users (Statista 2016b). Popular Apps include "WhatsApp" with 1 billion active monthly users, "Facebook Messenger" with 900 million, and "QQ Mobile" with 853 million monthly users (Statista 2016a). Each App can store user data in varying formats, and reverse engineering the extracted data can be difficult, and will likely remain an issue for forensic analysis of user data remnants.

Cloud Storage is also reportedly increasing (Quick and Choo 2013b), and many mobile phone apps store user data using this medium, rather than storing data on the device, with some apps having quite minimal data, such as the Microsoft Band and Health App retaining data for only a short time until the data can be moved to the Cloud storage account associated with a user, whereupon it is quickly removed from the mobile phone. With the growth in cloud storage there is a further avenue for data to be stored by users, which results in data accessible to a device or computer being far greater than the physical capability of the storage capacity. Terabytes of data are globally accessible to devices, and criminal users can use cloud storage to hide data from immediate view on a device which is not connected to storage media, although there are data remnants on computers and devices (Quick et al. 2014)

3.3.1 South Australia Police—Electronic Evidence 2000–2015

In 2009, Turnbull et al. examined data from South Australia Police (SAPOL) Electronic Crime Section (ECS) which showed a growth in requests for analysis of electronic evidence, including a growth in mobile phones for the period 2006–2009 (Turnbull et al. 2009). Updated data from SAPOL ECS covering the period 2000–2015 is listed in Table 3.2.

The data per financial year (01 July to 30 June) has been divided into categories according to the device type; portable devices encompassing **mobile phones** and tablets, **computers** and laptops, **storage** media such as USB storage, and **Other** types, such as CCTV. The data showed a growth on average of **60% per year for mobile phones**, and in 2005 the number of mobile devices represented approximately 9.6% of the property items, which grew to 69.4% of the property items in 2015. The data is charted in Fig. 3.2 and visually highlights the growth in mobile devices presented for analysis since 2006.

3.3.2 FBI Regional Computer Forensic Labs 2006–2013

To determine if the growth observed in the SAPOL ECS data is reflected in other jurisdictions, data from the Federal Bureau of Investigation (FBI) Regional Computer Forensic Labs (RCFL) Financial Year Annual Reports was examined (FBI_RCFL 2003–2012). The data in relation to the RCFL mobile telephone examinations is listed in Table 3.3. According to the 2009 Annual Report, a self-service process was introduced, termed cellular telephone kiosk (CPIK) resulting in the RCFL mobile phone examinations dropping from previous years. In the 2011 Annual Report, the

Table 3.2 Devices presented for analysis per year (2000–2015) (SAPOL ECS)

FY	Total cases	Mobile phones	Computers	Storage	Other	Total devices
2000	40					48
2001	140					226
2002	175					301
2003	197					341
2004	269	140	271	87	15	513
2005	273	59	452	93	13	617
2006	268	103	425	52	13	593
2007	402	578	422	61	44	1105
2008	548	851	488	76	72	1487
2009	661	1177	536	92	98	1903
2010	700	1115	543	151	102	1911
2011	872	1484	695	176	100	2455
2012	1014	1867	1042	337	164	3410
2013	1203	2273	810	343	173	3599
2014	1226	2517	774	342	141	3774
2015	1417	2846	766	363	135	4110
Total	9405	15013	7226	2173	1070	26393

Fig. 3.2 SAPOL ECS—Devices presented for analysis per Year (2004–2014)

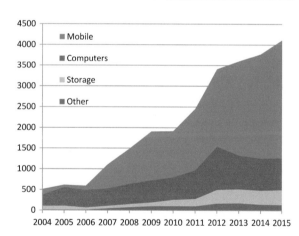

number of CPIK examinations is listed, and in the 2012 and 2013 Annual Reports, this also includes a process whereby local investigators remotely connect to the RCFL in a process termed Virtual Cell Phone Kiosk (VCPK) and when Loose Media is examined (LMK). On average, there is growth observed over this period of **81% per annum for mobile telephone examinations**.

Terrorist and organised crime groups are highly skilled in using technology to enable their activities at a global and local level, contributing to their ability to separate

Table 3.3 Mobile telephone examinations per year (FBI RCFL)

Annual report	Mobile phones	Comment
2006	701	Examinations
2007	1486	Examinations
2008	2226	Examinations
2009	1953	CPIK process introduced
2010	1909	Examinations
2011	8553	CPIK, LMK, VCPK
2012	13566	CPIK, LMK, VCPK
2013	15452	CPIK, LMK, VCPK

their activities. Many computers and devices are seized in relation to associated investigations, whereby digital forensic specialists extract and process the data from seized devices and computers, and provide the data to investigators for review. An example of this is the electronic evidence presented at the trial of the 2013 Boston Marathon bombing suspect Dzhokhar Tsarnaev, which consisted of mobile sync backups of text message communications, system files, documents, audio files, and twitter data (Burke et al. 2015). Tsarnaev was subsequently convicted in relation to the bombing. Other digital forensic data and information can also include data extracted from applications such as Twitter and other communication methods such as that used by terrorist groups (The_Australian 2015).

3.4 IoT Devices

The term "Internet-of-Things" (IoT) is used to describe the multitude of interconnected devices able to communicate with each other, offering benefits and applications to users as they become pervasive throughout society (Oriwoh et al. 2013). Devices can range from connected cars, fridges, smart homes, Christmas lights, fitness bands, kettles, and toasters, to early warning tide measuring buoys, air monitoring balloons, and other devices (Cassidy 2014). The volume of data generated from these devices can be large, and in consumer related devices, such as wearable technology, the data can be rapidly transferred from the source device to a connected mobile device, then quickly transferred to cloud storage, accessible using web-based applications designed to visually represent the data to users in an easy to understand manner (Huang 2016).

IoT devices can range from basic sensors, to sophisticated devices, which can potentially be commandeered for criminal use (Hegarty et al. 2014). The data on these devices or "things" varies according to the device, and can be unstructured, structured, or a combination. Data of potential forensic relevance can be sourced from a variety of devices, with potential implications for digital forensic identification, preservation, collection, analysis, and presentation (Hegarty et al. 2014; Oriwoh et al. 2013).

Data from a device can be used to prove or disprove information and circumstances, such as the examination of data on a fitness watch, which assisted in solving an investigation into a reported rape (Snyder 2015). IoT devices could be considered to be non-human witnesses with a range of varying information and observations. Identifying, collecting, interpreting, and presenting the data from IoT devices are some of the issues that need to be addressed. Further consideration needs to be made in relation to instances where there are multiple disparate devices, which individually may not progress an investigation, but when data from a variety of devices is merged, data particularly relevant to an investigation may become apparent.

Information and logs from IoT devices can provide investigation related data which may lead to identification of a person of interest. The perennial and often contentious issue, of putting a person at a keyboard, perhaps may be answered by an IoT device with biometric information linked to a person of interest wearing or using a device. A fitness device may potentially identify a person via biometric information, such as the heart rate of a wearer. Some fitness bands have GPS tracking capability, which may assist in providing information a person was at a location of interest, or alternatively provide information they were somewhere else.

Smart homes with security systems that monitor when a person enters or leaves the house or a room may be able to identify a user from fingerprint or biometric scanned data. Within a smart home, this may be linked to air conditioner and heating systems, providing further information relevant to the movement of a witness or suspect within a dwelling. The data may be stored on a device within the smart home, or transmitted to cloud storage associated with the device manufacturer, resulting in a further layer of identification, collection, preservation, and analysis, including jurisdiction issues when collecting data which may be stored interstate or overseas.

Other issues with IoT devices include legal issues, privacy, and security concerns (Oriwoh et al. 2016). One proposed method to forensically monitor IoT devices is the Forensic Edge Management System (FEMS), which is a proposed device which manages security of smart homes, and collects data of potential forensic value (Oriwoh and Williams 2014). However, not all IoT devices are constrained within smart homes. Hence, traditional identification, preservation, analysis, and presentation stages of digital analysis still need to be able to cope with a variety of IoT data and devices, without necessarily relying on an additional layer of forensic devices, data, and software, which may not be present in all situations (e.g. smart cars and wearable technology).

With the growing number of disparate devices, digital forensic practitioners will have a need to collect specific targeted data, not necessarily device specific, as relevant data may be on an IoT device, mobile phone, personal computer, smart home security system, or have been transferred to cloud or fog computing storage. There is a growing need to collect and examine data from a wider scope of devices and information storage, with a focus on the data which enables those involved in an investigation or probe to make a decision with as much relevant data as is available, in a timely manner.

3.5 Discussion

The ongoing growth of computers, mobile devices, IoT devices, and digital forensic data, provides a potential for far greater understanding of terrorist organisations and organised crime groups, however, there is a need to reduce the volume for storage and intelligence review purposes. A successful data reduction strategy can enable intelligence practitioners to access and review the information being collected and extracted in a timely manner. The storage demands for the FBI RCFL 20PB of data would cost many millions of dollars. The time to search this volume of data would potentially make the process futile, and it would take many years to manually review and comprehend the overall information holdings, let alone drill down to information of value.

The DRbSI data reduction process outlined in Volume 1 outlines a data reduction method demonstrated to reduce the overall volume data to that which has potential intelligence and evidential information. In the case of computers and storage media, using Data Reduction by Selective Imaging (DRbSI), results in a subset of information containing data with a large potential for relevance, and discarding data and files with a low potential of value. Initial experiments with mobile phone extracts demonstrated that mobile device extract data can be reduced by storing spreadsheet extract reports and XML formatted data exports, along with DRbSI subsets of exported video and picture files (further discussed in Chap. 4).

Experiments with test data and real world data (Vol. 1) demonstrated the ability to reduce data volume to 0.206% of the source. As an example, one case comprised 8.57 TB, and was able to be reduced to 12.3 GB. Further experiments with real world data demonstrated an ability to potentially reduce 12,000 mobile device extracts to 3.9 GB (see Chap. 4). Also using the DRbSI method would enable pictures and videos from 12,000 devices to fit onto a 320 GB hard drive.

Preliminary testing to examine the intelligence data potential of the DRbSI data subsets was undertaken with test data, loading many hundreds of device extract subsets into NUIX software, whereby it was possible to review and gather valuable intelligence from a large range of disparate case data, answering many research questions in regard to growth in devices, operating systems, and trends over time. Further application of this method could include the use of other intelligence and data mining software, such as Intella and IBM i2, to traverse and index the data contained within the subset files. This would potentially enable intelligence analysts to search on entity information, keyword filters, and other such refining tools to gain an understanding across a large variety of cases. Further application potential relates to entity extraction and relationship charting techniques, which has the potential to quickly inform an intelligence practitioner of linkages between vastly disparate cases.

The use of index and review methodologies could enable a fast scan for new and emerging crime typologies, such as the growth in the use of a particular communication medium, or common website addresses used across cases. Reports could be prepared based on keywords for intelligence probe typologies, such as; terrorism, organised crime, etc. This information could be further enhanced with the addition of other intelligence and data sources, such as; call charge records, intelligence reports (intreps), arrest reports, traffic stops, and also open source information such as Facebook, Twitter, etc.

Various types of intelligence product can be improved by the addition of digital forensic intelligence information. Tactical Intelligence supports front line staff and investigators, and is often tied to a specific investigation leading to an arrest or gathering evidence, mainly short term focussed activity directed to front line operational officers. Operational Intelligence sits at a broader organizational level to support area commanders and regional managers in crime reduction activity. This is a mid-level focus to assist with tackling organised crime groups, and for decision makers to determine the priorities for limited resource allocation. Strategic Intelligence aims to provide an understanding into patterns of criminal behaviour and the criminal environment, with a focus on potential future activities and longer-term resource allocation by upper management (Ratcliffe 2007). Strategic analysis is aimed at higher level decision makers, with a longer term focus (UNODC 2011).

Tactical intelligence usually has a focus on persons of interest, with dissemination via intelligence products such as target packages, person profiles, and relationship charts. These all can benefit from an analysis of digital forensic data holdings, whereby associates or specific persons may have information linkages across a wide variety of devices and data. Keyword searches can be used to locate particular information provided it is able to be undertaken in a timely manner. Relationship charts can be used to identify linkages and associations, using software such as NUIX, which provides this functionality. This information can be merged with other data holdings, and contribute intelligence to the products mentioned.

Operational intelligence usually has a focus on a crime group, such as gangs or organised individuals, usually at a local service area level, or with some cross-border linkages, and also at a higher level of organisation. Again, products can include target packages and relationship charts, and also intelligence reports and other briefing tools. Digital forensic data holdings can also contribute to operational intelligence, by searching across large volumes of subset data, including mobile device extracts, for a range of persons and associate entities, enabling an analyst to build a greater picture of an organisations spread, such as terrorist groups and organised crime groups. Merging digital forensic intelligence with other intelligence holdings can greatly expand the totality of understanding.

Strategic intelligence has a higher level focus, such as crime trends, and changing crime and communication methodologies. As an example, a strategic intelligence probe could examine and determine what communication methods are being used by large organised crime groups, such as common encryption techniques used across devices, or particular software or mobile application growing in usage. This knowledge can enable high level decision makers to determine where to focus resources, and also assist digital forensic specialists in knowing where to look for data and information across cases. By reviewing the data holdings from digital forensic analysis, high level trends can be observed and reported to upper management, including trends over time. Intelligence estimates can be prepared with a sound understanding of the data supporting intelligence for decisions.

There is a potential to significantly increase base knowledge and intelligence from the information currently held in digital forensic case files. Drawing together this volume of data can enable an intelligence analyst to gain an understanding of disparate information in a rapid manner, with minimal equipment and data storage demands. Terrorist organisations and organised crime groups thrive due to their method of siloed operation. Important data may be located on computers and mobile devices, and goes un-noticed in property rooms and case files. Intelligence analysts with the ability to step back and see the forest from individual trees, with a review across a wide variety of information holdings, may lead to a breakthrough in an understanding of the scope of an organisation, and the bring together currently unknown linkages.

Many agencies have the resources and equipment to deploy this process without costly equipment and training. Common forensic tools such as Guidance Software EnCase, X-Ways Forensic, and others, in conjunction with common intelligence and review tools such as; Nuix, i2, or Intella, are already in common use by various agencies. Applying a data reduction method such as Data Reduction by Selective Imaging can enable the reduction of a vast volume of data as subsets to address the growing volume of digital forensic data, enabling a capability to process and review this information in a timely manner. Processing and indexing the forensic data subsets enables the ability to search across a vast range of case and device data, and further software functionality enables the ability to understand the data at a wide-ranging level, and drill down to uncover disparate linkages between previously thought to be unrelated cases. This method is potentially a low-cost or no-cost solution which may lead to the solving of crimes, and potentially avert terrorist and organised crime activity.

3.6 Conclusion

There is a growing volume of computer and mobile device data seized and analysed by a wide range of agencies. Many of these devices and computers are used extensively for terrorism and organised crime, with their siloed activities aided by communication and information dissemination and dis-information, potentially enabling and promoting a wide range of crimes. Many devices are seized by agencies, but much of the data sits in property rooms and case files, underutilised for intelligence probes and estimates. The volume of data is growing, and many agencies struggle with storage, processing, and reviewing this information.

Current research has proposed a method to reduce data volume to reduce storage demands and review purposes, with a potential benefit for intelligence analysts. There is a need to harness this important data, and inform intelligence personnel of the potential value of the information holdings. Harnessing digital forensic data, by reducing storage demands and applying software solutions to index and extract entity information, such as Intella, NUIX and IBM i2, can lead to a greater understanding of cross-case disparate information. The next chapters focus on analysis of subsets of data from mobile devices and from other source data relating to a range of cases types encompassing many terabytes of source data, to formulate a method to rapidly locate evidence and intelligence from large data repositories of digital forensic data holdings.

The proposed forensic data reduction methodology uses currently available technology, and many agencies may already possess the software, training, and skills to deploy it. It is potentially easily implemented with minimal expenditure and effort. Intelligence analysts have an opportunity to lead the way, by applying their time-honed skills in reducing vast amounts of information to distilled points of relevance, and apply intelligence analytical skills to the digital forensic realm. The proposed methodology has application across the various intelligence functions; strategic, operational, and tactical. Agencies are standing on the crest of a tidal wave of data, which can be harnessed to prevent being drowned in the possible deluge.

3.7 Summary

In this chapter, the potential for intelligence from digital forensic data holdings was explored, which, in conjunction with digital forensic data subsets has potential benefits, including the need to harness this important data and inform intelligence personnel and investigators of the potential value of data contained within digital forensic information holdings.

In the next chapter, the process of data reduction of mobile phone and portable device extracts is examined. This serves to expand the potential application of the data reduction and quick analysis process to a wide variety of devices, hardware, software, and information formats, and explores the potential to gather intelligence from a range of disparate sources, as outlined in this chapter.

References

All URLs were last accessed (and correct) on 5 November 2016

Abraham, T. (2006). Event sequence mining to develop profiles for computer forensic investigation purposes. In *ACSW Frontiers'06: Proceedings of the 2006 Australasian workshops on grid computing and e-research*, pp. 145–153.

ACC (2013a). *National Plan to Combat Cybercrime*, Canberra.

ACC (2013b). *Board of the Australian Crime Commission, Chair Annual Report 2012–2013* Commonwealth of Australia.

Al-Zaidy, R., Fung, B. C. M., Youssef, A. M., & Fortin, F. (2012). Mining criminal networks from unstructured text documents. *Digital Investigation, 8*(3–4), 147–160.

Alink, W., Bhoedjang, R. A. F., Boncz, P. A., & de Vries, A. P. (2006). XIRAF—XML-based indexing and querying for digital forensics. *Digital Investigation, 3*, Supplement, no. 0, 50–58.

Bell, C. (2006). Concepts and possibilities in forensic intelligence. *Forensic Science International, 162*(1), 38–43.

Bettini, C., & Riboni, D. (2015). Privacy protection in pervasive systems: State of the art and technical challenges. *Pervasive and Mobile Computing, 17,* 159–174.

Burke, A., Corpuz, M., & Gans, F. (2015). *Jury presented with electronic evidence in Tsarnaev trial,* updated 24 March, 2015, The Daily Free Press, viewed 4 July, http://dailyfreepress.com/2015/03/24/jury-presented-with-electronic-evidence-in-tsarnaev-trial/.

Case, A., Cristina, A., Marziale, L., Richard, G. G., & Roussev, V. (2008). FACE: Automated digital evidence discovery and correlation. *Digital Investigation, 5,* Supplement, no. 0, S65–S75.

Cassidy, A. (2014). *The "Internet of Things" Revolution and Digital Forensics,* updated February 18, nuix, viewed 3 May, http://www.nuix.com/2014/02/19/the-internet-of-things-revolution-and-digital-forensics.

FBI_RCFL 2003-2012, *FBI Regional Computer Forensic Laboratory Annual Reports 2003–2012,* FBI, Quantico.

Garfinkel, S. (2006). Forensic feature extraction and cross-drive analysis. *Digital Investigation, 3,* Supplement, no. 0, 71–81.

Garfinkel, S. (2010). Digital forensics research: The next 10 years. *Digital Investigation, 7,* Supplement, no. 0, S64–S73.

Harrison, W., Heuston, G., Morrissey, M., Aucsmith, D., Mocas, S., & Russelle, S. (2002). A lessons learned repository for computer forensics.

Hegarty, R., Lamb, D., & Attwood, A. (2014). Digital evidence challenges in the internet of things. In 2014, *Proceedings of the tenth international network conference (INC 2014).*

Huang, J. (2016). *Extracting my data from the Microsoft band.* Retrieved April 27, 2016, from http://jeffhuang.com/extracting_my_data_from_the_microsoft_band.html.

IDC (2014b) *Worldwide smartphone shipments top one billion units for the first time,* international data corporation (IDC). Retrieved August 17, 2014, from http://www.idc.com/getdoc.jsp?containerId=prUS24645514.

ITU (2010). *The World in 2010, ICT Facts and Figures,* International Telecommunication Union (ITU), Geneva, Switzerland. http://www.itu.int/ITU-D/ict/material/FactsFigures2010.pdf.

ITU (2014) *The World in 2014, ICT Facts and Figures,* International Telecommunication Union, Geneva, Switzerland. Retrieved August 17, 2014, from http://www.itu.int/en/ITU-D/Statistics/Documents/facts/ICTFactsFigures2014-e.pdf.

Lexar (2016). *Press releases| Lexar,* SD Card Release Dates, Lexar. Retrieved April 20, 2016, from http://www.lexar.com/about/newsroom/press-releases.

Nykodym, N., Taylor, R., & Vilela, J. (2005). Criminal profiling and insider cyber crime. *Digital Investigation, 2*(4), 261–267.

Oriwoh, E., Jazani, D., Epiphaniou, G., & Sant, P. (2013). Internet of things forensics: challenges and approaches. In *2013 9th International conference on collaborative computing: networking, applications and worksharing (Collaboratecom),*

Oriwoh, E., & Williams, G. (2014). Internet of things: The argument for smart forensics: Handbook of research on digital crime, cyberspace security, and information assurance, p. 407.

Oriwoh, E., al-Khateeb, H., & Conrad, M. (2016). Responsibility and non-repudiation in resource-constrained internet of things scenarios.

OpenSignal (2014). *Android fragmentation report August 2014.* Retrieved August 23, 2014, from http://opensignal.com/reports/2014/android-fragmentation/.

Quick, D., & Choo, K-K. R. (2013b). Forensic collection of cloud storage data: Does the act of collection result in changes to the data or its metadata? *Digital Investigation, 10*(3), 266–277.

Quick, D., Martini, B., & Choo, K.-K. R. (2014). *Cloud storage forensics.* Syngress: An Imprint of Elsevier.

Ratcliffe, J. (2007). *Integrated intelligence and crime analysis: Enhanced information management for law enforcement leaders* (2nd ed.). Washington, DC: Police Foundation.

Raghavan, S., Clark, A., & Mohay, G. (2009). *FIA: an open forensic integration architecture for composing digital evidence: Forensics in telecommunications, information and multimedia* (pp. 83–94). Heidelberg: Springer.

Ribaux, O., & Margot, P. (2003). Case based reasoning in criminal intelligence using forensic case data. *Science and Justice, 43*(3), 135–143.

Ribaux, O., Walsh, S., & Margot, P. (2006). The contribution of forensic science to crime analysis and investigation: Forensic intelligence. *Forensic Science International, 156*(2–3), 171–181.

Ribaux, O., Baylon, A., Roux, C., Delémont, O., Lock, E., Zingg, C., et al. (2010). Intelligence-led crime scene processing. Part I: Forensic intelligence. *Forensic Science International, 195*(1–3), 10–16.

Rogers, M. (2003). The role of criminal profiling in the computer forensics process. *Computers and Security, 22*(4), 292–298.

SanDisk (2016). *Press Releases,* SD Card Release Information, SanDisk. Retrieved April 20, 2016, from https://www.sandisk.com.au/about/media-center/press-releases.

Shaw, E. (2006). The role of behavioral research and profiling in malicious cyber insider investigations. *Digital Investigation, 3*(1), 20–31.

Snyder, M. (2015). *Police: Woman's fitness watch disproved rape report*, updated 19 June, abc27 News, viewed 27 April, http://abc27.com/2015/06/19/police-womans-fitness-watch-disproved-rape-report/.

Statista (2016a). *Most popular global mobile messenger apps as of April 2016, based on number of monthly active users (in millions)*, Statista. Retrieved April 20, 2016, from http://www.statista.com/statistics/258749/most-popular-global-mobile-messenger-apps/.

Statista (2016b). *Number of apps available in leading app stores 2015*, Statistic. Retrieved April 20, 2016, from http://www.statista.com/statistics/276623/number-of-apps-available-in-leading-app-stores/.

Turnbull, B., Taylor, R., & Blundell, B. (2009). The anatomy of electronic evidence; quantitative analysis of police e-crime data. In *ARES '09. international conference on availability, reliability and security*, pp. 143–149.

The_Australian (2015). *Alleged Anzac Day plotters were groomed from frontline* Australia. http://www.theaustralian.com.au/in-depth/terror/alleged-anzac-day-plotters-were-groomed-from-frontline/story-fnpdbcmu-1227311119275.

UNODC (2011) United nations office on drugs and crime—Criminal intelligence manual for analysts, United Nations, New York, Vienna, Austria.

van Asten, A. C. (2014). On the added value of forensic science and grand innovation challenges for the forensic community. *Science and Justice, 54*(2), 170–179.

Walsh, S., Moss, D., Kliem, C., & Vintiner, G. (2002). The collation of forensic DNA case data into a multi-dimensional intelligence database. *Science and Justice, 42*(4), 205–214.

Weiser, M., Biros, D. P., & Mosier, G. (2006a). Development of a national repository of digital forensic intelligence. In *Proceedings of the conference on digital forensics, security and law*.

Weiser, M., Biros, D. P., & Mosier, G. (2006b). Development of a national repository of digital forensic intelligence. In Glenn S. Dardick (Ed.), *Editor-in-Chief Longwood University Virginia, USA*, p. 5.

Wiles, J., Alexander, T., Ashlock, S., Ballou, S., Depew, L., Dominguez, G., Ehuan, A., Green, R., Long, J., & Reis, K. (2007). Forensic examination in a terabyte world. In *Techno security's guide to e-discovery and digital forensics*. Elsevier, pp. 129–146.

Xu, Z., Liu, Y., Xuan, J., Chen, H., & Mei, L. (2015a). Crowdsourcing based social media data analysis of urban emergency events. *Multimedia Tools and Applications*, 1–18.

Xu, Z., Wei, X., Luo, X., Liu, Y., Mei, L., Hu, C., & Chen, L. (2015b). Knowle: a semantic link network based system for organizing large scale online news events. *Future Generation Computer Systems,. 43*, 40–50.

Xu, Z., Liu, Y., Yen, N. Y., Mei, L., Luo, X., Wei, X., et al. (2016). Crowdsourcing based description of urban emergency events using social media big data. *IEEE Transactions on Cloud Computing, 99*, 1–1.

Chapter 4
Data Reduction of Mobile Device Extracts

In the previous chapter, the process of quick analysis of data subsets and full forensic images was detailed. This next chapter examines the process of data reduction and analysis of mobile phones and disparate devices.

Mobile devices are increasingly becoming the focus of criminal investigations, such as those used by organised crime and terrorist groups (Burke et al. 2015; Corera 2015; The_Guardian 2015; WMNAGreenwood 2015). This growth has contributed to an increase in the volume of digital forensic data (Quick and Choo 2014a; Turnbull et al. 2009). Mobile device forensics is a relatively new field of digital forensics, and whilst processes to extract data are addressed by commercial offerings, such as MSAB XRY, Cellebrite UFED, and Oxygen Forensic Suite, the various tools output the extracted data in differing formats. Across a criminal or civil investigation, there may be a variety of devices to be examined, and the use of a multiple tools, methods, and processes may be required to extract and analyse data. This can lead to issues with extraction, analysis, and presentation, in a timely and efficient manner when the extracts are in differing formats (Grispos et al. 2011; Jansen and Ayers 2007; Turner 2005).

In recent years, social networking services for both individual (e.g. Facebook and LinkedIn) and enterprises (e.g. Yammer) are increasingly popular. This is partly due to the ongoing growth in the number of mobile devices, internet connectivity and the volume of data stored on these and other portable devices. Evidence from the investigation of social networking services (e.g. social networking apps) can include call and contact information to show relationships, SMS and MMS messages to substantiate communication, and picture and video data to show evidence of crimes or other breaches of legislation or policy. In addition, sensors in mobile devices can collect data relating to a user's location, environmental temperature, noise levels, motion, and biomedical information (Ye et al. 2012).

The information contained within mobile devices can answer the important questions of an investigation or probe, including; who, how, what, why, when, and where.

Material presented in this chapter is based on the following publication:
Quick, D. and Choo, K.-K.R., 2017. Pervasive social networking forensics: intelligence and evidence from mobile device extracts. Journal of Network and Computer Applications, 86, pp. 24–33.

49

D. Quick and K.-K. R. Choo, *Big Digital Forensic Data*, SpringerBriefs on Cyber Security Systems and Networks, https://doi.org/10.1007/978-981-13-0263-3_4

In the future, we may see embedded smart health devices in a person transmitting information to a mobile device for transmission to health specialists, resulting in information being stored on a device or in the cloud (Dar et al. 2014). This information may provide value to an investigation, such as identifying a suspect, or highlighting the health impact to a victim during a crime. Current commercial forensic solutions extract available data, and allow for exports and reports to be produced from the data. The extracted data, exported files, and reports, are growing in volume, influenced by the growing storage volume, growing data type, and number of devices.

In addition, there is a range of information available on mobile devices of great interest to intelligence practitioners. This can include; communications with other person/s, photographs, videos, audio recordings, documents and spreadsheets, emails, data remnants in applications, instant messaging chat, Facebook, Twitter, and other social media messages and data, geolocation data, metadata, contacts and phone call information. The volume of information on a typical mobile device nowadays can potentially be overwhelming, and therefore there is a need to be able to focus on information and data which may be of interest.

If this data was also available to search and review for intelligence information, in a timely manner, there is a potential to locate dispersed information which may assist with current and historical investigations, and build a knowledge base for future investigations and intelligence probes. However, this has historically been problematic due to the large volume of data, which is increasing at a substantial rate (Garfinkel 2010).

4.1 Digital Forensic Intelligence Analysis

Digital Forensic Intelligence Analysis is a process of applying Criminal Intelligence Analysis methodologies to Digital Forensic data. To visualise the process, in Fig. 4.1 the steps from the Intelligence Analysis Cycle (UNODC 2011) and the Digital Forensic Analysis Cycle (Quick and Choo 2013a) are merged to form the Digital Forensic Intelligence Analysis Cycle (DFIAC). The steps include; Commence (Scope/Tasking), Prepare, Evaluate and Identify, Collect, Preserve and Collate, Analyse, Inference Development, Present, Complete/Further Tasks identified. Both the Intelligence Analysis Cycle, and the process of Digital Forensic Analysis are cyclical, as is the DFIAC, in that it is an iterative cycle whereby a practitioner doing analysis may uncover information relating to another mobile device, and return to a process of preparation, evaluation, identification, collection, preservation, and collation for the new device and data.

In the field of mobile device forensics, there are a number of commercial solutions to extract and analyse data, such as; MSAB XRY, Cellebrite UFED, Radio Tactics ACESO, Access Data MPE+, Paraben Forensic, Oxygen Forensic, and CellXtract. Tassone et al. (2013) undertook experiments to compare three commercial forensic mobile phone extraction tools, and concluded that "no single tool can be solely relied upon to collect and present every item of potential evidence from a smart mobile

Fig. 4.1 Digital forensic
intelligence analysis cycle
(Adapted from Quick and
Choo 2013a, UNODC 2011)

device." This highlights that in a criminal or civil investigation, where multiple devices are crucial to a case, differing tools and methods may be needed to extract and analyse data from a variety of devices.

With the growth in the use and reliance on mobile devices, there is a growing need to gather and understand evidence, information, and intelligence from a wide variety of these devices. Phones and other mobile devices have the potential to provide important information, such as communications, geolocation information, associations, and timeline evidence. Developments in the convergence of information, coupled with devices containing a range of new sensor types, such as RFID, compass, GPS location tracking, health monitoring, and others, is leading to more and more divergent information and data on devices about user behaviour (Conti et al. 2012).

As an example of the volume of data on devices, data extracted from a test device; a 64 GB iPhone 5S, extracted using MSAB XRY 6.13, resulted in a 37.6 GB XRY extract file. This was exported to 37.2 GB of extracted files and reports. An iPad with 256 GB of storage would potentially contain up to 60 DVD's of information. This highlights the potential data available for analysis. When multiple types of these devices with increasingly larger data volumes are seized and presented for forensic analysis, there is a large potential volume of data available for analysis.

Along with the growth in the number of devices, there are multiple tools and methods to enable forensic extract and analysis of portable devices. Investigations often involve the extraction and analysis of many mobile devices. When a large number of persons are involved in a network, there can be a corresponding large number of devices to analyse, often requiring different forensic solutions and methods to extract data.

When undertaking an extract from a device, there are occasions when multiple methods are needed to gather relevant information. This can involve extraction via various methods, such as; Backup, Agent, Physical, and Logical, which refer to the method used to access and extract data. As an example; a Backup extraction involves using a device's operating system to initiate a backup and the forensic software then processes the backup file/s, whereas a Physical extraction involves accessing the device storage directly, bypassing the operating system on the phone. In addition, there may be other sources of phone data, such as iPhone, Windows Phone, or Android backups on a computer hard drive. This can result in multiple extracts for one device, with differing information in each extract.

4.2 Mobile Phone Extracts

This chapter examines the data output type from a variety of tools to determine opportunities for intelligence analysis processes to be applied, with a focus on the data export formats available across the various tools. The software utilised[1] included; MSAB (formerly Micro Systemation AB) XRY, Cellebrite UFED, Oxygen Forensic, Guidance Software EnCase, Paraben Forensic, and Magnet Forensic IEF. Each tool was used to access a range of test data extracts, and then export data in the various options available for each tool. As the capabilities of each tool varies, the focus was to explore a generic method to export data and to determine if there is a common export format which would enable the various extract types to be merged for intelligence and evidence analysis purposes.

The test data used for the research included; mobile phone test data extracts from the Digital Forensic Corpus (Garfinkel et al. 2009b), data extracts available from the Oxygen Forensic website (Oxygen 2015), and data extracted as part of previous cloud storage research (Quick and Choo 2013c, 2013d; 2014b; Quick et al. 2014). This research focuses on methods to reduce large volumes of disparate extracted data, and methods to export data to a common format. Methods for forensically extracting phones are not examined, nor is this a comparison of the capability of the various tools, as the focus of this research is the intelligence analysis potential across a variety of devices.

The research focus is on the export potential of the various software tools, and is not intended to be a comparison of the capability of each tool (for a comparison of tools see Tassone et al. 2013). To examine the data output potential of each of the mobile phone forensic tools, test data available for each tool was used, as these contained a wide variety of data, rather than using a limited number of available mobile phones and extracting the same data using a variety of tools. A wide variety of disparate data exists in the extracts. This section outlines the data exports available for each of the

---

[1] Selection was based on the hardware/software the author had access to. No personal recommendations or endorsement should be presumed from the tools selected.

tools examined; MSAB XRY, Oxygen Forensic Suite, Cellebrite UFED, EnCase 7, Paraben, and Magnet Forensic Internet Evidence Finder.

4.2.1 MSAB XRY 6.12.1

For this research, the process of exporting data using test data files from previous research (Quick and Choo 2013c, 2013d; 2014b; Quick et al. 2014). These consisted of a range of extracts from a 16 GB Apple iPhone 3G which were undertaken using MSAB XRY 6.3, each resulting in average of 12.8 GB per XRY file. The available export formats from XRY include; PDF, DOCX, XLSX, and XML formats. Each test file was opened and the data was exported using the options available in XRY 6.12.1. Eight (8) test data file exports resulted in an average file size of 40 MB for the PDF report, 117 MB for the DOCX report, 768 kB for the XLSX file, and 20 MB for the XML export.

The spreadsheet exports contained information about the files from the device, as did the XML exports. The XML format has potential to provide for a common export format, which could be used to merge and examine output from a variety of tools. The total volume of the mobile phone extracts was 99.4 GB, and the equivalent XLSX files totalled 7 MB. The exported XLSX reports comprised the extracted and parsed information from a range of data sources including Contacts, Calls, Messages, Chat, and other Application data. The exported files included pictures and videos which may be relevant in some cases. Using a process of thumbnailing video files was beneficial in reducing the volume of the exported video whilst retaining a reference to the contents of each video file suitable for intelligence purposes. Using a process of picture dimension reduction was beneficial in reducing the volume of the exported pictures whilst retaining a capability to view the picture contents.

4.2.2 Oxygen Forensic Suite 6.4.0.67

A variety of mobile device extracts are available from the Oxygen website in the Oxygen OFB format (Oxygen 2015). These are compressed in a Zip container format, and can be expanded using unzip software. The original size of the devices is not listed in the extract or on the website, and a comparison could not be made to the original size of the device. Each test file was opened and the data was exported in the various options using Oxygen Forensic Suite 2014 version 6.4.0.67. From the eleven (11) test data file exports resulted in an average file size of 31 MB for the PDF report, 11 MB for the RTF report, 3.6 MB for the XLS file, and 2.6 MB for the XML export.

The total volume of the OFB files was 3.7 GB, and when unzipped to the original extracts totalled 4.8 GB. The XLS files totalled 129 MB, and the exported XML files totalled 39.1 MB. Examining the various exports highlighted that the XLS format, which included call and message information, also included thumbnails of pictures. Other extracted data in the XLS spreadsheets included; Browser Activity, Map information, iOS call logs, Email, SMS and MMS messages, Instagram, KiK, and Parsed Search Queries. As in the XRY tests, the process of picture reduction conducted on the exported files from the device extracts resulted in smaller storage requirements for the exported files, which can enable faster processing of volumes of data due to smaller file sizes.

4.2.3   Cellebrite UFED 3.9.2.4

The Digital Forensic Corpus (Garfinkel et al. 2009b) includes a number of extracts which appear to be from a Samsung GSM-I9020a Nexus S obtained using Cellebrite UFED 1.1.9.4 in July 2012. The extracts are available in zip format, and unzip to the full UFED binary file extracts. The zip file sizes range between 118 and 190 MB (totalling 791 MB), and each unzip to approximately 15.3 GB of data each, totalling 92.0 GB. The unzipped binary files were processed using UFED Physical Analyzer 3.9.2.4 and exported to available report formats, including; PDF, DOCX, XLSX, and XML. From six (6) test data file exports resulted in an average file size of 12 MB for the PDF report, 247kB for the DOCX report, 218 kB for the XLSX file, and 1 MB for the XML export.

Examining the various reports highlighted that the spreadsheet (XLSX), and XML reports were the smallest relative size which contained the information that may be relevant to an investigation or intelligence probe. Whilst the total volume of the DOCX reports were marginally smaller, the XLSX reports were useful for intelligence analysis to remain consistent with the report types saved from other mobile phone forensic tools in this research.

4.2.4   Guidance Software EnCase 7.09.04

Included in the Digital Forensic Corpus (Garfinkel et al. 2009b) are file extracts from an Apple iPhone which appear to be from EnCase forensic software, saved in a logical container (L01) format. Each test file was opened and the data was exported in the various options using EnCase 7.09.04. There were five (5) test data files comprising 92.7 MB in L01 files, which when exported resulted in average file size of; 14.7 MB for the PDF report, 21 kB for the TXT report, 5.3 MB for the RTF report, 8.5 kB for the CSV file, and 32.8 kB for the XML export.

Examining the various exports led to the conclusion that the Spreadsheet (CSV) files were the smallest format which included contacts, calls, message and Application information. The XML format has potential to provide for a common export format able to be used to examine output from a variety of tools.

4.2.5   *Paraben Device Seizure 6.66*

Paraben Device Seizure 6.66 was used with extract files from an iPhone and from an Android phone, in Paraben DS format totalling 1.6 GB. Each test file was opened and the data was exported in the various options using Paraben 6.66 Software. Of the two (2) test data files, when exported resulted in average file size of; 3.67 MB for the PDF report, 6.9 MB for the TXT report, 253.8 MB for the HTML report, 14.2 MB for the CSV file, and 1.2 MB for the XML export. The file volume of the exported files was approximately 2.9 GB, and the equivalent XLS files totalled 14.4 MB, or 4.18 MB when saved as XLSX files.

Examining the various exports highlighted that the XLS files were the smallest format which included contacts, calls, message, web bookmarks, and application information such as Kik and TextFree. The XML format has potential to provide for a common export format able to be used to examine output from a variety of tools.

4.2.6   *Internet Evidence Finder (IEF) 6.4.2.0070*

In the Digital Forensic Corpus, there are mobile device extract files in the E01 format, which appear to be AccessData MPE+ extracts (Garfinkel et al. 2009b). These files were viewed using FTK Imager 3.2.0.0, and the data within each container was extracted. Minimal information was located, mainly consisting of JPG picture files. These were exported and dimension reduced to 800 x 600 pixels using XnView 2.35 software, which reduced the file volume from 51.5 to 2.5 MB.

The E01 files were then examined using Magnet Forensics Internet Evidence Finder (IEF) 6.4.2.0070 and report outputs produced. From the nine (9) test data files, when exported resulted in average file size of; 58.9 MB for the PDF report, 157 MB for the HTML report, 1.76 MB for the CSV file, 120 MB for the XLS file, and 13.9 MB for the XML export.

The volume of the mobile phone export files was 203 GB, and the equivalent CSV files totalled 14 MB. Examining the various exports highlighted that the CSV files were the smallest format which included contacts, calls, messages, emails, Gmail, web bookmarks, and other application information. A data reduction process applied to the file output using a process of thumbnailing the video files and reducing the dimensions of the exported pictures reduced the volume of the overall data export size, resulting in 253 MB of data (Documents and reduced dimension pictures) from a 1.6 GB export size, resulting in a total of 364 MB of subset data from the 203 GB total, reducing to 0.179% of the original volume. This represents the extracted and parsed contents of the phones, and enables processing and analysis of the data in a timely manner.

Table 4.1 Total data volume for the exported test data

	Source/files (GB)	Container size (GB)	XLS or CSV (MB)	XML (MB)
MSAB XRY	128	99.4	6.062	162.5
Oxygen	4.8	3.7	129.3	39.1
Cellebrite	1.076	1.082	1.307	6.259
EnCase 7	0.0857	0.0927	42.5	164.2
Paraben	2.92	1.684	14.4	2.36
IEF	203	3.2	14	111
Total	339.9 GB	109.2 GB	207.6 MB	485.4 MB

4.2.7   Summary of Mobile Phone Exports

Using the test data, the various options to export data in a variety of formats from EnCase, FTK Imager, Cellebrite UFED, MSAB XRY, IEF, Oxygen, and Paraben were examined. Table 4.1 displays the data volumes from each tool used to process the test data, and the totals across the devices. Overall, observations related to a volume reduction from a total of 339.9 GB to 207.6 MB in spreadsheets (CSV, XLS, or XLSX), and 485.4 MB for XML files, representing the exported and parsed data including contacts, calls, messages, emails, Gmail, web bookmarks, GPS coordinates, and a range of other application information.

In an investigation, there may be a potential need to conduct analysis across a number of devices, which may require multiple software solutions to extract data. As an example, the SAPOL ECS data has many cases with ten (10) or more devices per request. Whilst the test data was able to be exported to variety of formats, the exports were in differing formats. Whilst the data was able to be exported to a range of formats; XLS/CSV, XML, HTML, PDF, or Google Earth GPS data, it should be noted each software solution when used to export data does this with different row and column types. To enable cross-device analysis, it may be necessary to align the columns and rows to enable merging the data to a single source, or analyse the data from multiple sources in a single software instance.

4.3   Digital Forensic Intelligence Analysis of Test Data

Using the exported reports from the test data, the process of gaining intelligence from data can be undertaken. Using the test data Spreadsheet exports, all the CSV, XLS, and XLSX export reports were collated and manually merged to align columns and combined into one (very large) spreadsheet of all data from the extracts. To undertake analysis, the combined spreadsheet data was then converted to Pajek data format and loaded into Pajek 64 software. A Fruchterman Reingold 2D entity link chart of was created, highlighting the interlinked nature of the 41 mobile device extracts (Fig. 4.2).

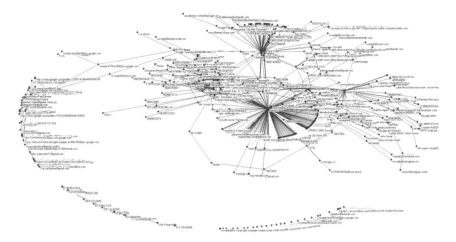

Fig. 4.2   Entity relationship chart of oxygen test data using Pajek 64 4.05

For an intelligence analysis probe, the focus could then be on the linkages and the person/s and communications, in an effort to gain an understanding of the persons involved in possible organised crime networks. An inference was then developed, in this case the analysis of the data indicated an organised network involving Patrick and Simon Payge.

Further analysis was then undertaken on test data exports in relation to the persons communicating in the network to determine their role. This was achieved by undertaking analysis of the communications (e.g. SMS and email messages), dimension reduced pictures, and other extracted data. Using the data located within the spreadsheet extracts and the knowledge gained from creating the Pajek chart, a summarised entity link chart was manually created (Fig. 4.3). This shows the links between persons in a possible (fictitious) organised crime network, highlighting the highly interconnected relationships between the persons using the various devices, which is a summary of the data in Fig. 4.2.

The information located on the devices can also be used to create detailed subject profiles of the persons in the network, for example summarising the extracted information relating to "Patrick Payge", or other persons. The intelligence gained from a link network analysis, such as this, may lead to an understanding of disparate linkages in a network, which were previously unknown. This intelligence would then be presented to the client, with a formal briefing and report provided. If further analysis was required, the process would return to the 'Prepare' stage with perhaps a new focus for information.

As a result of the test data experiments, it is concluded that there is potential benefits when exporting data to a common format, and a process to reduce the volume and processing demands of mobile device extracts, by:

1. exporting the extracted data as spreadsheet (XLS/CSV/XLSX),

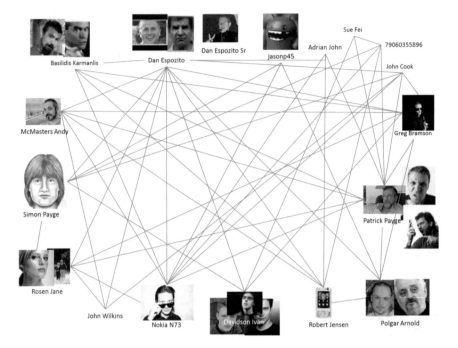

Fig. 4.3 Entity link chart of oxygen mobile device test data extracts

2. exporting pictures, videos, documents, and other files, and applying the digital
   forensic data reduction process, reducing the dimension of pictures, and thumbnailing video files.

   Examining data from a wide range of devices potentially enables evidence analysis
and intelligence probes to be thorough and improve knowledge and understanding.
There are also potential benefits to building strategic knowledge when information
of a wide range of devices can be examined for trends, such as the growth in popular
operating systems, and other information of value to high level strategic decision
makers.

4.4 Review of South Australia Police Data

With a view to applying the digital forensic intelligence analysis process to real
world data, access to case data of South Australia Police Electronic Crime Section
was made possible. XRY file metadata information was examined, without viewing
the contents of the devices or extracts, focussing on the file metadata for the XRY data
extracts. The goal of this was to determine the strategic intelligence (designed for
upper level management decision making) that could be gained from the metadata, as

Table 4.2 SAPOL XRY extract size 2013–2015

Year	Number	Total volume (GB)	Average extract size
2010	4	18.7 MB	4.675 MB
2011	24	621 MB	25.875 MB
2012	145	38.6 GB	266 MB
2013	506	169 GB	335 MB
2014	250	374 GB	1.5 GB
2015	265	738 GB	2.8 GB

opposed to case specific intelligence. Log entries of a selection of XRY extracts were identified and collected, focussing on the extract time and metadata. The file size of the XRY extract files was collated and reviewed, including the size of the XLSX exports, export folder volume, all without viewing the actual user data contained within the files.

4.4.1 Data Volume of South Australia Police XRY Extracts

In the analysis of the data across 1,348 current XRY files, the total volume of the XRY files totalled 1.36 TB. This equates to an average of approximately 1.009 GB per extract. The source data files were referenced from financial year 2011 to financial year 2015, representing the financial year of device seizure (01 July to 30 June). 169 of these XRY files had been exported to XLSX, and these XLSX files totalled 55 MB, an average of 325 KB per extract. 52 of the XRY files had been exported to files in folders, totalling 47.9 GB, representing an average of 921 MB for each export. When examining XML output, there were only 25 XRY exports which had been exported to XML, totalling 297 MB, from 20.6 GB of XRY files, or 0.144% of the volume, and an average of 11.8 MB per device.

Extrapolating the observed file sizes, the conclusion is that there is potential to reduce the data volume of many thousands of devices to a small volume. Approximately 12,000 devices could be reduced to 3.96 GB of spreadsheet XLSX files containing; communication information, SMS and MMS messages, phone calls data, contact information, chat messages and content, and a range of information. This data could be indexed using intelligence analysis software such as; Nuix, i2 Analyst's Notebook, or Intella PI. The processed data would then be available to be searched, or entity link charts created across a range of device extracts. The evidence and intelligence information across a large number of devices could be invaluable to current and future investigations, with a potential to locate cross case intelligence relating to organised crime or terrorism investigations. The average size of a selection of XRY extract files for the years 2010–2015, is listed in Table 4.2. This data shows an increase in average from 4.7 MB in 2010 to 2.8 GB in 2015, and supports the data in Table 3.1 relating to the increase in data volume of devices.

Table 4.3 SAPOL ECS
average extract times
2010–2015

Year	Average extract time (minutes)
2010	1.5
2011	11.9
2012	9
2013	27
2014	48
2015	52

Table 4.4 Reported mobile
device data storage capacity
(SAPOL XRY metadata)

Year	8 GB	16 GB	32 GB	64 GB	128 GB	Total devices
2012	4	6	2	2		14
2013	1	4	2	3		10
2014	2	9	5	3		19
2015	1	13	7	4	1	26
Total	8	32	16	12	1	

4.4.2 Extract Time from South Australia Police XRY Data

The metadata in the log files in relation to the time to undertake the extract of data
from a device using XRY was also examined. The data from XRY extract files ranging
from 2010 to 2015 was compiled, listed in Table 4.3. The data related to 57 devices,
and showed an average time in 2010 of 1.5 min, to an average extract time of 52 min
in 2015. The devices seized in 2014 took approximately 48 min on average to extract,
with the longest being 2 h. The devices seized in 2015 took approximately 52 min
on average to extract, with the longest being 3 h. It was also observed that a 16 GB
device took approximately 35 min to extract, a 32 GB device took approximately
39 min, and a 64 GB device was approximately 97 min.

To further explore the potential to gain strategic intelligence from a large volume of data, XRY Spreadsheet (XLSX) files from 738 devices, totalling 370 MB,
were loaded into NUIX 4.2.3. These were processed and indexed in approximately
15 min. A search for the term 'Storage Capacity' resulted in 69 entries across the
738 extracts. Examining the values reported for device storage capacity, the data was
compiled in Table 4.4. From this information, it is apparent that 16 GB devices have
the highest number, and larger devices are increasingly presented for processing.
However, drawing conclusions from this information is difficult due to the limited
amount of data from the sample set.

Searching the 738 indexed device reports for the term "Device Name" resulted
in 244 matches for phone or mobile devices. The extracted device manufacturer
and model information is listed in Table 4.5. From this data, it is clear that Nokia
devices, which were popular in 2013, have dropped off over this time period, and
Apple, Samsung, and Android devices have increased. However, again, the limited
data makes it difficult to draw firm conclusions in relation to the number and types of

Table 4.5 Device name from XRY (SAPOL XRY metadata)

Years	Apple iPhone	Apple iPad	Nokia	Samsung	Android generic	Sony Ericsson	LG	Others	Total
2011			4	1		1	1		7
2012	12	2	13	3	1	2	2	1	36
2013	12	3	23	12		1		4	55
2014	23	4	13	12	11	4	2	8	77
2015	19	5	6	17	10		2	10	69
Total	66	14	59	45	22	8	7	23	244

devices over this time, but serves to highlight the strategic level information available from an indexed volume of data subset information.

4.4.3 Summary of South Australia Police Data

From the data examined, the exported data for a large number of devices could be stored as spreadsheet XLSX files with a potential storage requirement volume of *giga*bytes rather than *tera*bytes. The data representing communication information, SMS and MMS messages, phone calls data, contact information, chat messages and content, and a range of information from applications, could be processed and reviewed for digital forensic intelligence and evidence analysis purposes, potentially uncovering disparate links across investigations if focussing on tactical or operational intelligence.

Processing the extracted data using indexing and analysis software highlighted the potential to apply a Digital Forensic Intelligence Analysis process to the extracted data for the purposes of strategic intelligence, i.e. discovering information of potential relevance to strategic management decision making, such as focussing resources to develop extract and analysis methodologies for particular device types, or determining storage requirements for subsequent years. Analysis of popular applications may also highlight trends in relation to user activity. Applying intelligence analysis methods would also be relevant for Operational and Tactical Intelligence purposes.

Applying a Digital Forensic Data Reduction (DRbSI) process to the exported pictures and videos further reduced the volume of data, potentially enabling the storage of dimension reduced pictures and video thumbnails in a smaller volume, further adding to the intelligence analysis potential of mobile device extract data. It was also observed that the average storage volume requirements of data exports have increased over the years, and the time to extract has also increased.

4.5   Discussion

The type of evidence or information which may be relevant to an investigation will vary according to the scope of the task. This could be a single item or multiple items, such as; SMS communication, pictures, video, audio recordings, chat, or application data. There may also be a need to determine associations between people, addresses, and communication devices. It is difficult to anticipate what an investigation will need from an extract or from a range of extracts, as this varies according to an individual investigation, or an overall intelligence probe. However, there may be some common needs across investigation types. For example, in a drug investigation, there may be a focus on communications, but pictures of a methamphetamine lab or unexplained wealth could be relevant (WMNAGreenwood 2015).

In a possession of child exploitation material (CEM) investigation, there may be a focus on pictures and videos, but communication may be relevant in relation to the grooming of victims (e.g. it is known that social networks had been used by child sex offenders to cultivate trust and form a bond or relationship with the victim with the purpose of sexual exploitation (Choo 2009; O'Connell 2003). A terrorism investiga- tion may encompass pictures, videos, communication, associations, documents, and a range of other data. An example of this is the electronic evidence presented at the trial of Dzhokhar Tsarnaev for the 2013 Boston Marathon bombing, which consisted of mobile sync backups of text message communications, system files, documents, audio files, and twitter data (Burke et al. 2015).

Relevant information can also include data extracted from applications, such as Twitter and other communication methods used by terrorist groups (The_Australian 2015). Hence, a Digital Forensic Intelligence Analysis process should collect a wide range of file and data types to encompass a variety of potential investigation and intelligence needs.

Distilling the various needs across investigations is difficult. The focus of this research was to explore the potential to collect relevant information from a range of mobile phone extracts. The process of collecting spreadsheet reports enables the collection of a wide range of information, such as communication, internet history, messages, contacts, and chat. The process of data reduction by collecting a range of potentially relevant file types, thumbnailing video, and reducing the dimension of pictures, further enabled the reduction of storage volume of files, picture, and video data from devices as a subset.

By reducing the storage demands of multiple device extracts, it becomes easier to manage, process, and analyse data for evidence and intelligence. Data from multiple devices can be examined using software such as; Nuix, Intella, i2 Analyst Notebook, IEF, or Forensic Phone Analyser (FPA). An example of gaining intelligence from a range of exported devices was outlined in this section when 738 mobile device spread- sheet exports were loaded into Nuix 4.2.3 and indexed in approximately 15 min. It became possible to quickly search the data to determine the reported storage capacity for a volume of devices, and other strategic intelligence as discussed.

Also highlighted was the process of loading test data subsets into Pajek software to produce an entity link chart (Fig. 4.2), and then add to this with information from the spreadsheet reports to build an intelligence entity chart (Fig. 4.3). This highlights the potential benefit to also search for keyword terms and build cross-case intelligence and evidence from a large number of devices.

The information contained within the spreadsheets and XML files can assist in cross-case and cross-device timeline analysis. As an example, in many investigations there is a need for a timeline of events to enable analysis. Using the date/time information from each device extract, it is possible to merge the information from many devices into a single listing, and undertake analysis on the merged data. Information can be sorted or filtered on the time/date, on the various information contents, such as; contact information, or key words in message content, or keyword searches can be conducted across devices.

In the experiments conducted on the test data, it was observed that the time formats varied across software and export types. As an example, the time could be reported in Universal Time (UTC), Local time, or an Offset (i.e. +9:30). The times recorded in various formats will potentially need to be converted to a common date and time format for analysis purposes. Some tools export in UTC, others according to the time setting on the analysis PC, and others presenting an adjusted time based on the internal phone setting and the time information stored in the phone. Manually adjusting the various exports can be time consuming, and is to be noted that this highlights a potential need for functionality within mobile device extract software to align the various time formats to a common time format.

Mobile devices can be an excellent source of digital forensic intelligence, which can assist with a wide range of investigation or intelligence probes, such as; terrorism, child exploitation, drug trafficking, homicide, fraud, computer crime, and other investigations. With more data and information available to be reviewed, a better understanding is possible, but with the growing size of data, storage and processing can become problematic. By reducing the data volume, it becomes easier to manage, and less time to process, enabling a better understanding in a shorter amount of time. In addition, merging the information from a variety of sources improves knowledge, such as from; mobile devices, computers, call charge record information, and other sources.

The ability to gather evidence and intelligence can relate to operational, tactical, and strategic topics of interest, such as; websites of interest, persons, addresses, mobile numbers, email addresses, and information holdings about persons of interest across a range of devices. The ability to locate this information can be crucial to investigations, and the ability to locate and visualise disparate data can lead to breakthroughs in current and future investigations.

4.6 Summary

When conducting investigation involving the use of social networking services, it is integral that forensic practitioners begin by identifying the means that will be used to locate and acquire evidence (e.g. mobile devices). The volume of data on mobile devices is increasing, and is predicted to continue in future years. A review of historical trends highlighted that there are nearly 7 billion global subscriptions for mobile devices, and this is increasing. Both iOS and Android operating systems are prevalent, and the storage volume of devices growing from 16 GB in 2007 to 512 GB in 2017. In a similar timeframe, MicroSD card storage has grown from 512 MB to 512 GB, and SD cards have grown from 1 GB to 1 TB, with the price per megabyte dropping significantly in the same time. There is a potential that in 10 years' time, portable storage will be up to between 512 TB and potentially 1 PB. Cloud storage data will also impact on the growing storage potential for users.

The volume of devices seized and forensically examined is also increasing, with growing backlogs of requests and devices awaiting examination. For example, there has been an average 60% per annum increase in requests for analysis of devices submitted to South Australia Police Electronic Crime Section, with 69% of all requests in 2015 relating to mobile devices, up from 10% on 2005. The FBI RCFL has also reported an increase of 81% in mobile phone analysis per annum.

It is possible to output extract data in spreadsheet and XML format using common extract solutions, which provides for this data to be processed for many thousands of devices. Using a process of exporting spreadsheet data it was demonstrated that it is possible to reduce the storage demands to enable multiple device analysis in a timely manner. Future research in relation to digital forensic intelligence analysis could involve the inclusion of data from forensic analysis of other devices, such as; computers, portable storage, GPS units, CCTV footage, cloud stored data, biomedical data, and Internet of Things (IoT) data. Another potential research opportunity is to explore the use of the XML data and develop software to automatically merge the output from various tools into a common format.

This research has also demonstrated a method to reduce the storage demand of a volume of data, which in the test cases reduced from 339.9 GB to 207.6 MB in spreadsheets. In the real-world cases, the volume for many thousands of devices would approximate a reduction from potentially *tera*bytes to *giga*bytes. This would potentially enable timely analysis review of a large volume of data, which may lead to breakthroughs in current and future investigations, and lead to solving a variety of cases. The application of a Digital Forensic Intelligence Analysis process can enable a better understanding of large volumes of data extracts, including disparate case data holdings.

The next chapter examines input of external source data with DRbSI subsets and device extracts to further improve the value of digital forensic data.

References

All URLs were last accessed (and correct) on 5 November 2016

Burke, A., Corpuz, M., & Gans, F. (2015). *Jury presented with electronic evidence in Tsarnaev trial*, updated 24 March, 2015, The Daily Free Press. viewed 4 July, http://dailyfreepress.com/2015/03/24/jury-presented-with-electronic-evidence-in-tsarnaev-trial/.

Choo, K-K. R. (2009). *Online child grooming: A literature review on the misuse of social networking sites for grooming children for sexual offences. Research and public policy No 103*, Canberra, ACT.

Conti, M., Das, S. K., Bisdikian, C., Kumar, M., Ni, L. M., Passarella, A., et al. (2012). Looking ahead in pervasive computing: Challenges and opportunities in the era of cyber–physical convergence. *Pervasive and Mobile Computing, 8*(1), 2–21.

Corera, G. (2015). *The MI5 spy in your mobile: How 7/7 London attack triggered new data-fed war on terror which led to capture of 21/7 bomb plotters which made ISIS vanish into encrypted web but makes your calls transparent to GCHQ spooks in 'Doughnut'*, updated 14 June 2015, http://www.dailymail.co.uk/news/article-3122808/How-7-7-London-attack-triggered-new-data-fed-war-terror-led-capture-21-7-bomb-plotters-ISIS-vanish-encrypted-web-makes-calls-transparent-GCHQ-spooks-Doughnut.html.

Dar, K., Taherkordi, A., Baraki, H., Eliassen, F., & Geihs, K. (2014). A resource oriented integration architecture for the Internet of Things: A business process perspective. *Pervasive and Mobile Computing*.

Garfinkel, S., Farrell, P., Roussev, V., & Dinolt, G. (2009b). Bringing science to digital forensics with standardized forensic corpora. *Digital Investigation, 6*, S2–S11.

Garfinkel, S. (2010) Digital forensics research: The next 10 years. *Digital Investigation, 7*, Supplement, no. 0, S64–S73.

Grispos, G., Storer, T., & Glisson, W. B. (2011). A comparison of forensic evidence recovery techniques for a windows mobile smart phone. *Digital Investigation, 8*(1), 23–36.

Jansen, W., & Ayers, R. (2007). Guidelines on cell phone forensics. *NIST Special Publication, 800*, 101.

O'Connell, R. (2003). *A typology of child cybersexploitation and online grooming practices*. Preston: University of Central Lancashire.

Oxygen (2015). *Demo Backups*, viewed 15 June, http://www.oxygen-forensic.com/en/download/devicebackups.

Quick, D., & Choo, K-K. R. (2013a). Dropbox analysis: Data remnants on user machines. *Digital Investigation, 10*(1), 3–18.

Quick, D., & Choo, K-K. R. (2013b). Forensic collection of cloud storage data: Does the act of collection result in changes to the data or its metadata? *Digital Investigation, 10*(3), 266–277.

Quick, D., & Choo, K-K. R. (2013c). Digital droplets: Microsoft SkyDrive forensic data remnants. *Future Generation Computer Systems, 29*(6), 1378–1394.

Quick, D., & Choo, K. (2013d). Dropbox analysis: Data remnants on user machines. *Digital Investigation, 10*(1), 3–18.

Quick, D., & Choo, K-K. R. (2014a). Impacts of increasing volume of digital forensic data: A survey and future research challenges. *Digital Investigation, 11*(4), 273–294.

Quick, D., & Choo, K-K. R. (2014b). Google Drive: Forensic analysis of data remnants. *Journal of Network and Computer Applications, 40*, 179–193.

Quick, D., Martini, B., & Choo, K.-K. R. (2014). *Cloud Storage Forensics*. Syngress: An Imprint of Elsevier.

Tassone, C., Martini, B., Choo, K-K. R., & Slay, J. (2013). *Mobile device forensics: A snapshot*. Australian Institute of Criminology

The_Australian (2015). *Alleged Anzac Day plotters were groomed from frontline* Australia, http://www.theaustralian.com.au/in-depth/terror/alleged-anzac-day-plotters-were-groomed-from-frontline/story-fnpdbcmu-1227311119275.

The_Guardian (2015). *French terrorism attack: suspect took selfie with severed head* updated 28 June 2015, The Guardian, France, http://www.theguardian.com/world/2015/jun/28/french-terrorism-suspect-took-selfie-with-slain-victim.

Turnbull, B., Taylor, R., & Blundell, B. (2009). The anatomy of electronic evidence: Quantitative analysis of police e-crime data. In 2009 *International Conference on Availability, Reliability and Security, ARES '09*, pp. 143–149.

Turner, P. (2005). Unification of digital evidence from disparate sources (Digital Evidence Bags). *Digital Investigation, 2*(3), 223–228.

UNODC (2011) *United nations office on drugs and crime—Criminal intelligence manual for analysts*, United Nations, New York, Vienna, Austria.

WMNAGreenwood (2015) *Drug dealer nabbed after posing with wad of cash*, updated 07 June 2015, Western Morning News, viewed 4 July, http://www.westernmorningnews.co.uk/Drug-dealer-nabbed-posing-wad-cash/story-26651154-detail/story.html.

Ye, J., Dobson, S., & McKeever, S. (2012). Situation identification techniques in pervasive computing: A review. *Pervasive and Mobile Computing, 8*(1), 36–66.

Chapter 5
Digital Forensic Data and Open Source Intelligence (DFINT+OSINT)

This chapter focuses on the externally sourced data aspect of the framework, and explores a process of data mining to extract entity information and a process of fusion with external source data to improve the knowledge discovery potential and intelligence from digital forensic data holdings.

The DRbSI and Quick Analysis process (Vol. 1 Chap. 4 and Vol. 2 Chap. 2) have potential applications for criminal intelligence purposes. In research testing, the ability to use DRbSI subsets and the Quick Analysis process with Bulk Extractor software (Garfinkel 2013) was explored to gain a rapid understanding of digital forensic data holdings. In this chapter, a process of value-adding to extracted data by drawing on OSINT resources is explored. This allows practitioners and intelligence personnel to add value to the data and information; thus, enabling a better understanding of the criminal environment.

The contributions of this chapter are:

- a process of semi-automated scanning of multiple digital forensic data subsets from a variety of devices, including computers, hard drives, mobile phones, portable storage, cloud storage, and Internet-of-Things (IoT) data, with a view to extract entity information; and
- value-add to the entity information by drawing on the resources of OSINT with a view to expanding cross-device and cross-case analysis, leading to improved overall knowledge relating to disparate cases.

In the next section, the background and related work for digital forensic intelligence (DFINT) and open source intelligence is outlined. The process of using DRbSI subsets in conjunction with semi-automated analysis to enable entity extraction and open source information searching is then discussed. Following this, the process of DFINT+OSINT analysis is applied to M57 test data to enable an understanding of its application, and then explore the application of the methodology to real-world data. The final sections discuss the research findings.

Material presented in this chapter is based on the following publication:
Quick, D. and K.-K.R. Choo, Digital Forensic Intelligence: Data Subsets and Open Source Intelligence (DFINT+OSINT): a Timely and Cohesive Mix, Future Generation Computer Systems, ISSN 0167-739X, http://dx.doi.org/10.1016/j.future.2016.12.032.

D. Quick and K.-K. R. Choo, *Big Digital Forensic Data*, SpringerBriefs on Cyber Security Systems and Networks, https://doi.org/10.1007/978-981-13-0263-3_5

5.1   The Role of Intelligence

The role of intelligence is to provide decision makers with independent and impartial information which is timely, accurate, relevant, verifiable, answers a question, and enables proactive decision-making (Gibson 2004). Criminal intelligence analysis is a term used to describe how information and intelligence can be used in the investigation of crime and persons involved or suspected of being involved in crime (UNODC 2011).

5.1.1   Intelligence-Led Policing (ILP)

The process of intelligence analysis is well entrenched within enforcement and other agencies, and includes a concept of "Intelligence led policing" (ILP), which is defined as;

> the application of criminal intelligence analysis as an objective decision-making tool in order to facilitate crime reduction and prevention through effective policing strategies and external partnership projects drawn from an evidential base. (Ratcliffe 2008).

ILP focuses on four elements, namely:

- targeting offenders,
- management of crime hotspots,
- linked crimes and incidents, and
- preventative measures.

Organised crime groups and terrorist organisations often consist of members with antecedents for the predilection of crime, and members often associate with persons with similar criminal background, but also draw on new recruits with limited criminal background. Organised crime was previously associated with the Cosa Nostra, but is nowadays quite different (UNODC 2011). Organised criminal groups now can have well-developed organizational structures, mainly established for obtaining power and/or wealth. Such groups include outlaw motorcycle gangs, Russian organized crime, Asian organized crime, African organized crime, drug cartels, and street gangs, such as; Asian, Korean, Hispanic, black, and white supremacy groups (UNODC 2011). It is reported that the complexity of these groups is increasing, with fluid structure-less networks, and increasing cooperation between different organized crime groups and networks (Choo 2008; Choo and Smith 2008; UNODC 2011).

Organised crime involvement now extends to; trafficking in human beings, drug trafficking, extortion, fraud, murder, and high-technology crime, facilitated with the growth in Internet resources, opening new opportunities for profit. The National Organised Crime Response Plan 2015–2018 of the Australian Government estimates that organised crime costs Australia $15 billion per annum in transnational crime, money laundering, identity crime, and the growth in technology facilitates this (Government 2015). The United Nations Office on Drugs and Crime (UNODC) has reported an "escalation of high-technology crime is a challenging and relatively new arena for law enforcement" (UNODC 2011, p. 8), and that organised crime groups are more sophisticated and dynamic than ever before (UNODC 2011). The UNODC clearly states that "the challenge for law enforcement is to be prepared for this increasing sophistication in order to reduce the impact of criminal activities on our communities" (UNODC 2011, p. 8). With the increasing volume, variety, velocity, and veracity of digital forensic data, there is an opportunity to focus and learn from the information contained within this data, with an appropriate method to process the data in a timely manner.

The aim of a criminal intelligence analyst is to gather information in relation to criminals and criminal enterprises, and prevent or disrupt crime and criminal activity. The focus should, therefore, be to develop useful sources of information, including details of associates and relationships between individuals and their role in a criminal enterprise (UNODC 2011). The pervasive nature of ICT has resulted in a vast amount of information on devices, and data transiting from devices via the Internet to be stored in cloud storage environments. The role of digital forensics is to identify, collect, and preserve digital data which may provide assistance in legal enquiries. This is not limited to evidence alone, and there is a role for digital forensics in criminal intelligence analysis, supported with open source and external source intelligence and information.

5.1.2 Open Source Intelligence

OSINT has been utilised by many agencies and contributes to strategic, operational, tactical, and technical intelligence needs (Gibson 2004). OSINT is potentially a cost effective and rapid source of information, and the information and intelligence derived can potentially be shared (Best 2008). OSINT involves information extraction from publicly available sources (e.g. social networking sites). The Internet is now a major source of information, with estimates that data volume will grow from 4.4 zettabytes (ZB) in 2013 to 44 ZB by 2020, doubling in size every two years (IDC 2014a). The digitalised society we are witnessing has led to the globalisation of commerce, and opportunities for the globalisation of crime. This is enabled by the ability to easily travel across borders and transit international distances with relative ease.

This growth in data requires software which can provide for rapid content discovery, search, and retrieval. The Internet itself is not a source, but the means to access information sources, which can include media monitoring services, specialist information sources, 'grey literature' such as academic papers, and satellite imagery (Gibson 2004). Care must be taken with OSINT as information in the public domain is not necessarily verified and may be biased or inaccurate (UNODC 2011). Identification of sources of information is an ongoing process, as different means of communication go through a cycle of popularity. Search engines such as Google, which enable searching web sources by crawling and indexing hosted content, are slow, but effective. Web mining tools that focus on specific sources can provide alerts to keyword terms when changes are made, or matches are located.

OSINT can be fast, flexible, dynamic, communicable, shareable, partner forming, can encompass rapid evaluation or in-depth analysis at strategic, operational, tactical, and technical levels, and identify and mitigate risk, i.e. from 'horizon scanning' to sophisticated targeting (Gibson 2004). One challenge with OSINT is the data source language and the need to translate the language, which may necessitate the use of a translation service, training for analysts, or the use of translation software (UNODC 2011).

Today's unparalleled access to global satellite data, coupled with Google street view pictures of a large percentage of populated environments, has provided for vast amounts of data and information. As this information is not classified, there are fewer barriers to information sharing, although the intelligence derived from OSINT may need to be classified. It is quite clear that data available via the Internet is potentially and currently the greatest data source ever available, and with the rapid rate that data is doubling, this is anticipated to only increase in future. The vast amount of data and information can assist with providing actionable intelligence to decision makers.

It is apparent that in today's connected world, with a vast volume of data a mere click of a mouse away, that criminals and organised crime groups will utilise new and sophisticated methods of communication. Hence, agencies tasked to investigate these groups have a need to gather information about activities undertaken in the digital realm, or with a digital footprint. Furthermore, with the growing number and storage capacity of mobile phones, computers, and portable devices increasing dramatically, there is a vast pool of information in relation to criminal activity.

The FBI has applied the process of criminal profiling to the digital offending realm, developing cyber-criminal profiles (Rogers 2003). However, this may not necessarily take into account the information available from victims' computer and devices, or the potential to develop psychological profiles of a wider range of crimes using the digital intelligence available from computers and devices, which when analysed can reveal a lot of information about the user.

A process of forensic feature extraction and cross drive analysis was first proposed in (Garfinkel 2006) and has been refined over the years to develop software to assist with processing and extracting entity information from digital media storage. The next step of this is to build on the extracted entity information, and again, an automated process is necessary, given the sheer volume of data and entities resulting from even small hard drive storage. Research in relation to the development of a method to value-add to the entity and information extracted is necessary, as is a method which is applicable in the current environment involving real-world cases and real-world data volume.

Beebe (2009) emphasised the need for research in crime network identification. The importance of applying intelligence analysis techniques to digital investigations was also discussed in Chap. 3 and this chapter continues this research focus by applying link analysis methods to digital forensic data and expanding on this with open source and external source information.

In Weiser et al. (2006) a repository of information is proposed to store information relating to digital forensic cases, to build a knowledge base of cases including a case tracking system that stores forensic discoveries related to a case, an expert system record of best practice, and certified tools index. This aspect of digital forensic intelligence appears to relate to a higher level focus to build a knowledge base, rather than a focus on the use of intelligence analysis techniques to assist with the process of digital forensic analysis.

In this research, the focus is on the merging of digital forensic analysis and intelligence analysis techniques to add value to the process of both digital forensics and intelligence analysis. A national repository knowledge base for digital forensic practitioners is an admirable goal, and with the appropriate security and controls, could be expanded to include intelligence extracted from digital forensic data, with the adoption of a suitable method of data reduction, such as that proposed in Vol. 1 Chap. 4.

5.1.3   Digital Forensic Intelligence + OSINT

With the vast quantity of data available from digital forensic analysis, there is a wealth of information which can be potentially improved with open source information to enable a better understanding of events or persons, and improve decision making opportunities. One issue affecting rapid and timely analysis of large volumes of digital forensic data is the growth in media volume and the associated increase in the time to undertake searches and review information. The proposed data reduction method in Vol. 1 Chap. 4 has enabled faster collection and processing of digital forensic data. This process of rapid extraction and analysis enables the processing of large volumes of digital forensic data in a timely manner.

In the next section, the proposed framework is outlined, with a goal of enabling the inclusion of open source information with digital forensic analysis to encompass building on the data that is extracted through digital forensic analysis, such as computer hard drives, mobile phones, tablets, media storage devices, IoT devices, and cloud stored data. Using the Data Reduction by Selective Imaging (DRbSI) data reduction process (Vol. 1 Chap. 4) (Quick and Choo 2016), and semi-automated entity information extraction (using Bulk Extractor software), a process of fusion with open source information is explored. The aim is to expand knowledge and intelligence from large volumes of data by a process of;

- digital forensic data reduction,
- semi-automated entity extraction, and
- external source OSINT searches.

In the proposed process for digital forensic and open source analysis, the information from a wide scope of devices and information storage is enhanced with open source intelligence. This is to enable those involved in an investigation or intelligence probe to make decisions with as much relevant knowledge as is available, in a timely

Digital Forensic Intelligence and Open Source Intelligence (DFINT+OSINT) Framework	
Commence	Outline focus and scope of investigation.
Prepare	Ensure correct equipment and expertise.
Identify and Collect	Identify devices with potential evidence/intelligence, photograph and document
Data Reduction by Selective Imaging (DRbSI)	Load forensic image, or connect write-blocked physical device. • Filter and select pre-identified DRbSI files; File and OS, Software, Internet History, User created Documents, Email, Pictures, Video, etc. • Deselect overwritten data and non-relevant files [if necessary, mount forensic image as logical drive/s] • Convert Video files to thumbnail/s (e.g. using mtn batch file) • Shrink Picture files [1024 or 800 pixels wide/high] and place into L01 • Export a File List to CSV and convert to XLSX or compress to ZIP Export selected files to L01 or other forensic container
Quick Analysis and Entity Extraction	Undertake analysis of the DRbSI Subset, processing the data holdings with various tools to extract data and information, such as; RegRipper for Registry Information, File Metadata, Bulk_Extractor, Internet Evidence Finder, NetAnalysis, etc.
Open Source Intelligence (OSINT)	Process and load the entity information into software, such as Maltego and undertake web searches using Zotero to capture, collate, and store data. Search other OSINT and External Source resources to gain a greater understanding of the Entity and extracted Digital Forensic data
Entity Chart	Process and Load the Entity information into entity charting software, such as Maltego or Pajek64
Inference Development	Develop hypotheses and inferences based on the information findings, producing intelligence product
Presentation	Produce written and/or verbal report of hypotheses, inferences, and findings
Complete	Finalise the matter, or identify further avenues of enquiry

Fig. 5.1 Digital forensic intelligence and OSINT framework (Step 7)

manner using the proposed digital forensic intelligence and open source information framework.

5.2   DFINT+OSINT Method

The proposed framework for the process of digital forensic intelligence and open source intelligence (DFINT+OSINT) is based on the digital forensic intelligence analysis cycle (Chap. 2) and the digital forensic data reduction methodology (Vol. 1 Chap. 4). The proposed DFINT+OSINT framework (Fig. 5.1) is outlined in this section.

When working with open source data for intelligence purposes, consideration should be made regarding the following points for each source: authority, accuracy, objectivity, currency, and coverage (Gibson 2004). The use of a rating system for intelligence and sources is also appropriate, such as the 4 × 4 system or 6 × 6 system (admiralty scale) (UNODC 2011).

As with any investigation or intelligence probe, timely and accurate notes of the steps undertaken should be maintained, and any information and evidence secured according to agency directions or industry best-practice (ACPO 2006; NIJ 2004, 2008) Legislation and legal authority must be checked and appropriate prior to commencing, and ensure compliance at all stages.

When working online, practitioners are advised to ensure identity protection measures are appropriate, and network security is paramount when dealing with source access via open Internet connections. Covert operations need to ensure the appropriate approvals and security is in place prior to commencing, as it potentially only takes one miss-step to jeopardise an operation or personnel involved, which in some cases may be life-threatening consequences.

Digital forensic analysis follows a well-established framework, namely: identification, preservation, analysis, presentation (McKemmish 1999). Intelligence analysis involves a similar process of collection, collation, analysis, and presentation. The Digital Forensic Intelligence Analysis Cycle (DFIAC) is a merger of the methodologies of digital forensics and intelligence analysis to form a process of Commence, Prepare, Evaluate and Identify, Collect, Preserve, Collate, Analyse, Inference Development, Presentation, Completion or Further Tasks Identified (Chap. 4).

Using the DFIAC to frame the process, a process of DFINT+OSINT is outlined as a sub-cycle of a wider Investigation or Intelligence probe, as follows:

Commence (Scope/Tasking): the focus, aims, and scope of analysis are outlined to enable preparation and guidance for the overall examination.

Prepare: gather the anticipated equipment required and expertise, including confirmation of legal authority, network security, and covert considerations.

Identify and Collect: identify devices with potential evidence and/or intelligence, and undertake appropriate physical examination and documentation, according to agency policy and procedures.

Data Reduction by Selective Imaging (DRbSI): collect a digital forensic subset of data from the identified device or media. This involves utilising the process outlined in Vol. 1 Chap. 4, i.e. connect the identified media, then run a filter for pre-identified files and data. If necessary, reduce the dimension of pictures, and thumbnail video data. Export a list of all files on the media, and export all this into a logical forensic container (e.g. L01, AD1, or CTR).

Quick Analysis and Entity Extraction: using the process of Quick Analysis and Entity Extraction as outlined in Chap. 2. The entity extraction process involves using software to process the various data types retained within the DRbSI subset, and merge the output into a single source of information. The use of software, such as Bulk Extractor, assists with extracting a range of key entity information.

OSINT: identify sources of data and potential evidence and intelligence, such as: data which may be on social media websites, global or local media reports, 'grey' literature, satellite images, Google Street view information, or other open source media. Once data or information source is identified, conduct searches for known relevant entities; names, addresses, email addresses, phone numbers, vehicle details, and other information pointers. If relevant data is located, then it should be forensically handled where possible, i.e. printed to PDF or use screen capture (Microsoft Windows Snipping Tool) or screen capture software. Further in-depth analysis of websites may be necessary, and may locate additional information not normally presented publicly, i.e. within HTML source code for websites. The preservation process can align with a data collection and reduction process, such as that outlined in Vol. 1 Chap. 4 to collate a subset of relevant data. The use of software, such as Maltego, may assist with bulk data analysis and retrieval.

Entity Chart: the identified and collected OSINT data is then included with other data subsets and data extracted from computers, mobile phones, Internet of Things (IoT) devices, including data from cloud stored providers, for examination for evidence or intelligence, with a focus of that of the scope of the task. If during the process of analysis, additional sources of data are identified (e.g. other social media websites, media reports, or cloud stored data), the process forks to the 'Preparation' stage to collect the new data, whilst the analysis progresses.

Inference Development: with the knowledge gained during the process of collation and analysis, ideas are formed in relation to the questions of who, how, what, when, why, and where. The gained knowledge is used to form inferences about the investigation or intelligence probe to answer questions or outline findings. The intelligence and source data should be rated using a rating system, such as the 4×4 system or 6×6 systems (UNODC 2011).

Presentation: the findings of the overall process of analysis are formed into a report (written and/or verbal) which is communicated to the requesting persons involved in the investigation, legal process or probe.

Complete: the matter is finalised, and data archived according to agency practice and procedures. If further tasks are identified, the process continues in the cycle until complete. As part of the completion process, feedback should be sought from the persons involved to ensure the scope of the task has been met, and also practitioners should provide feedback to those involved in the task to ensure they are aware of the findings, and/or their role in the overall process.

5.3 Results: Digital Intelligence and OSINT from M57 Test Data

The growth in the volume and number of devices encountered in investigations has resulted in a need to collect and analyse growing volumes of digital forensic data in a variety of formats. The test data from the M57 corpus (Garfinkel et al. 2009) as previously used for digital forensic data reduction research, and successfully reduced the volume of data to 0.206% using the DRbSI process (Vol. 1 Chap. 4). A process of Quick Analysis was then outlined in this Volume to distil relevant information from the digital forensic data subsets. Subsequent to this, the digital forensic data from the test data (M57) computers, portable storage, mobile phones, and tablet devices, and source data comprising approximately 498 GB was merged. This was successfully reduced to 4.25 GB of DRbSI subsets and logical container files encompassing potentially relevant information.

A bulk data analysis process was applied to the data subsets, using semi-automated entity extraction from the forensic subsets using Bulk Extractor 1.5.5 software (Garfinkel 2013). This scanned the DRbSI data subsets, and the output encompassed 2.02 GB, comprising 23,496 email features, and 22,962 picture files, in approximately 30 min. Mobile phone extracts from 41 mobile devices, comprising 207 MB, were merged into a single source file for analysis.

The data output from the Quick Analysis process which included parsing the Windows Registry files, Internet Evidence Finder, NetAnalysis software, and information extracted from a variety of data sources within the DRbSI subsets, was merged with the output from Bulk Extractor, along with the previously merged mobile phone extracted data, resulting in a very large file of extracted entity information with associated source and relationship links. This was loaded into Pajek64 software.

This process has encompassed the first five stages of the DFINT+OSINT framework (Fig. 5.1), and now moves to the next stage, by using the extracted single-source entity information with Maltego CE to explore the process of expanding knowledge of the persons and entities contained within the data by locating available OSINT relative to the M57 test data.

A guide to OSINT analysis from (Toddington_International 2016) is summarised as:

- Choose an effective search tool,
- Use extended search capabilities (GREP),
- Search deep web resources, such as; databases, electoral roles, telephone, business databases,
- Review LinkedIn, Facebook, Twitter, YouTube, Flikr, Instagram, PhotoBucket, web blogs, Tripod, online sales sites, such as; eBay, Gumtree, Craigslist, Whirlpool,
- Run WHOIS searches for domain names,
- IP addresses (extracted from Registry and Internet History), genealogy sites, maps, traceroute, wayback machine, review source HTML, trace emails,
- Search for names, usernames, account names, email, phone numbers, addresses, family members, friends, associates, image EXIF data, GEO DATA,
- Use Zotero to collect, collate, and store data as you go, and
- Use snipping tool or print to pdf.

Also, notes should be made of the searches conducted, including; keyword search terms used, which websites were examined, any email references, personal information, associates, online images, chat, social network, further avenues of enquiry, time and date, and importantly, legal authority to undertake the analysis.

The extracted entity information from the test data was loaded into Maltego CE, displayed in Fig. 5.2. This chart shows the interlinked nature of the disparate data sources and entities extracted from the M57 corpus DRbSI subsets.

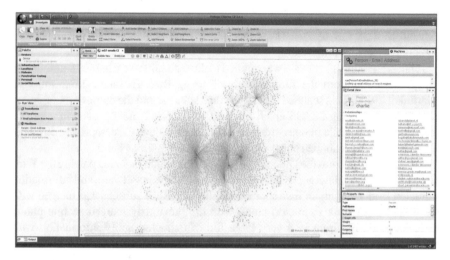

Fig. 5.2   Test Data loaded into Maltego CE

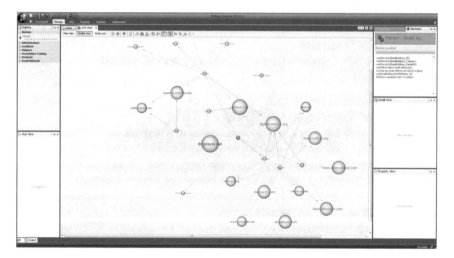

Fig. 5.3   OSINT URL references displayed in Maltego CE

Maltego Transform searches of the entities within the link chart were undertaken (Fig. 5.3). This resulted in a large amount of data matches, expanding knowledge in relation to the entities in the test data, and included URL locations with references to the email addresses and entities contained within the M57 corpus.

A selection of the URL matches located with OSINT is listed in Table 5.1. These show the type of external source data located which relates to entities contained within the extracted data from the DRbSI subsets. In a rapid and timely manner it was possible to add-value to the information in relation to the M57 data, expanding the knowledge-base with information available from open sources. Using this

Table 5.1 OSINT URL references located with Maltego CE

Name	URL
Jean	http://maj3sty.tistory.com/1034
Jean	http://maj3sty.tistory.com/category/%5B+%5D%20Forensic?page=8
Jean	http://www.doc88.com/p-1836912450568.html
Charlie	http://simson.net/ref/2012/2012-08-08%20bulk_extractor%20Tutorial.pdf
Alison	http://www.tuicool.com/articles/eiYNzuU
Jo	http://www.osdfcon.org/presentations/2015/McCarrin-Allen_osdfcon.pdf
Pat	http://digitalcorpora.org/downloads/bulk_extractor/BEUsersManual.pdf

process, digital forensic intelligence in conjunction with open source information has expanded knowledge. Whilst this increased information and knowledge-gain is of benefit in research, more importantly, this type of information and intelligence building can greatly assist in real world investigations.

5.4 Applying DFINT+OSINT to Real World Data

From the research outlined earlier, the entity information extracted from the M57 test data is similar to that which is extracted from real world data. The volume in real world data holdings is often much larger, which can result in longer search times. However, with more data there is better information potential.

There is also an opportunity to develop a method of refining the data and entities to that which relates to a case, and exclude or filter out generic data that exists in many operating systems and software installations, such as Microsoft Windows URL and email links for help and assistance. There is potentially a large volume of entities which can be excluded as these are unlikely to be related to an investigation. Undertaking a bulk extraction of a newly installed operating system and software and using this as a source of 'known-good' entities, which can then be used to remove these 'known-good' entities from real world data, would enable a further reduction in the number of entities for OSINT research. The use of the National Software Reference Library (NSRL) hash databases is also of potential benefit to further reduce the volume of entities extracted.

With real world data, data from IoT devices such as fitness bands which record GPS locations of the wearer may be relevant, and can include instances where it is uploaded to cloud storage. Security systems such as smart door locks which record biometric information as a person enters or exits a smart home could also be relevant, as is wireless internet connected doorbell systems with video recording capability which record movement of persons near the device. Data from these systems can be extracted and merged with the digital forensic data for analysis, and provides for even more information for investigators and analysts to examine. Hence, a process of data reduction, quick analysis, and external source intelligence can be beneficial to those involved in an investigation to understand the context of the information available.

By adding value to the information contained within digital forensic data, there is an opportunity to explore cross-case intelligence analysis, which in real-world cases may highlight cross-case linkages which were previously unknown to investigators. Indeed, the first author has experience where case linkages were unknown to disparate investigations due to the different focus of the various investigations, i.e. drug importation investigations and local service area property crime offending, and when the cross-case linkages have been brought to the attention of the separated investigation teams, this has enabled a better understanding of the volume of disparate (but actually connected) offending.

By implementing a method of building a knowledge base of cases, such as that proposed by Weiser et al. (2006), there is an opportunity to assist with disparate cross-case linkages being discovered early enough in an investigation to ensure appropriate resourcing of investigations, with a potential for a more timely resolution of cases. This must be balanced with appropriate security of the information, and legal authority to access and review the data.

In the previous research, the metadata contained within archived cases from South Australia Police Electronic Evidence Section data backup archives was examined (Volume 1 and 2). The content of case data was not examined, and only reviewed the times and data from processing of limited archived meta-data.

One archived case examined comprised eighteen computers, laptops, portable storage, mobile phones, and tablet devices, totalling 2.7 TB of source data. The volume of data was reduced according to the DRbSI process outlined in Vol. 1 Chap. 4, resulting in 46.1 GB of DRbSI subsets. Full imaging took approximately 42 h, and the DRbSI process took less than 4 h. To test the use of a semi-automated analysis process, the subsets were batch processed with Bulk Extractor 1.5.5 software, processing in 1 h 19 min. In comparison, processing the original source data took 43 h and 11 min. As per the process undertaken with the M57 data, it would be possible to merge the output entity information for further analysis with Maltego and adding value to the information with OSINT data analysis (this process was not undertaken with this data).

In addition, the DRbSI subsets from 544 archived devices were loaded into NUIX 6.2.3, EnCase 6.19.7, and EnCase 7.10.5. Again, the data was not viewed, rather, the times for processing was noted. EnCase 6.19.7 took approximately 3 min to load and open the 544 L01 files. File signature analysis was run, and took 2 h and 8 min. Over 10 million files were presented for analysis, including 907,015 documents, 52,742 emails, 2,221,521 picture files, and 2,333 container files. Within this data was potentially relevant entity information which could be improved with OSINT data.

The subsets when loaded into NUIX 6.2.3, provided for metadata analysis, which included strategic intelligence analysis to identify the types of phones presented for analysis, identifying that mainly iPhone and Samsung mobile phones were present. This highlighted that research into the device storage of these devices is warranted as they appear to be quite popular in relation to other devices. Further device specific information was not viewed. In addition, a focus on the JPEG EXIF metadata highlighted that Panasonic, Nikon, and Canon camera identifiers were present (further analysis was not undertaken on this data).

This research demonstrated a capability to process DRbSI subset L01 files from real-world devices ranging from USB storage to multi-terabyte hard drives, and it was possible to load and process these with EnCase 6.19.7, EnCase 7.10.5 and NUIX 6.2.3, and a potential to conduct further analysis of the data using Bulk Extractor across the subsets which could be further enhanced with Maltego to locate any open source information relating to the entities. Further analysis of the data was not undertaken due to privacy considerations.

5.5 Discussion

As outlined, the literature review highlighted a need for further research in the use of intelligence analysis techniques with digital forensic data. A corpus of test data was collected to undertake experiments, and from this it was possible to determine a method to undertake in-depth analysis to value-add to the entity information present in digital forensic case data. This is encompassed in the proposed DFINT+OSINT framework. Aspects of this framework were applied to real world data, which indicated the potential application to real world cases. In this manner, intelligence from DFINT+OSINT data has been enhanced.

Criminal intelligence is described as a national asset, which should be; "collected once and used often for the benefit of many and therefore adds value to the decision-making process" (Australia 2013, p. 62). This principle is also applicable to digital forensic data, and the analysis of disparate case data can have benefits to society in solving and progressing cases in a timely manner. As IoT devices, computers, portable storage, mobile phones, and tablet devices become more pervasive throughout society, there will be a growing need for forensic analysis of these devices. With the growing volume of disparate data, there is a need to be able to undertake analysis on growing volumes of structured and unstructured data. The method outlined in the previous sections as applied to test data (M57) and real world data, demonstrated an ability to undertake analysis of a large volume of disparate data, and locate potential evidence and intelligence.

In experiments, it was possible to scan data-reduced subsets in a semi-automated manner, and then merge the output to enable the examination of a large volume of data in a timely manner for linkages across devices and cases. As more and more devices are seized and presented for digital forensic analysis, there will be a larger source of data for criminal intelligence analysis, potentially locating evidence and intelligence to enable investigators and decision makers a better understanding of events from large volumes of data. Strategic and management level information can be drawn from digital forensic data; operational knowledge can be located and provided to investigators and managers, including information relating to crime trends. Tactical, target specific information can also be located and communicated in a timely manner.

By enhancing the information contained within digital forensic data by undertaking semi-automated analysis of entity information with open source data sources and information, there is an opportunity to fast-track investigations, and locate disparate linkages, which may otherwise remain unknown.

5.6 Summary

This chapter explored the aspect of external source data, which addresses Step 7 of the framework (Fig. 1.1). The process enables a fusion of open source (via the Internet) and closed and confidential source (digital forensic subsets) data sources. The use of semi-automated data mining software and external source collection software enabled the rapid processing of disparate case data to improve the knowledge discovery and intelligence potential of digital forensic data holdings.

References

All URLs were last accessed (and correct) on 5 November 2016

ACPO (2006). *Good practice guidelines for computer based evidence v4.0*, Association of Chief Police Officers. Retrieved March 5, 2014, from www.7safe.com/electronic_evidence.

Australia Co (2013). *Parliamentary joint committee on law enforcement inquiry into the gathering and use of criminal intelligence*, Canberra.

Best, C. (2008). Open source intelligence. *Mining massive data sets for security: Advances in data mining, search, social networks and text mining, and their applications to security, 19,* 331–344.

Beebe, N. (2009). Digital forensic research: The good, the bad and the unaddressed. In *Advances in digital forensics* (pp. 17–36). Springer.

Choo, K.-K. R. (2008). Organised crime groups in cyberspace: a typology. *Trends in organized crime, 11*(3), 270–295.

Choo, K.-K. R., & Smith, R. G. (2008). Criminal exploitation of online systems by organised crime groups. *Asian Journal of Criminology, 3*(1), 37–59.

Garfinkel, S. (2006). Forensic feature extraction and cross-drive analysis. *Digital Investigation, 3,* Supplement, no. 0, 71–81.

Garfinkel, S., Farrell, P., Roussev, V., & Dinolt, G. (2009). Bringing science to digital forensics with standardized forensic corpora. In *DFRWS 2009, Montreal, Canada.* Retrieved September 9, 2009, from http://digitalcorpora.org/corpora/disk-images.

Garfinkel, S. (2013). Digital media triage with bulk data analysis and bulk_extractor. *Computers and Security, 32,* 56–72.

Gibson, S. (2004). Open source intelligence: An intelligence lifeline. *The RUSI Journal, 149*(1), 16–22.

Australian Government (2015). *National organised crime response plan 2015–2018*, Australia. https://www.ag.gov.au/CrimeAndCorruption/OrganisedCrime/Documents/NationalOrganisedCrimeResponsePlan2015-18.pdf.

IDC (2014a). *The Digital Universe of Opportunities: Rich Data and the Increasing Value of the Internet of Things*, EMC Corporation. Retrieved June 1, 2014, from http://www.emc.com/leadership/digital-universe/2014iview/executive-summary.htm.

McKemmish, R. (1999). *What is forensic computing?*

NIJ (2004) *Forensic examination of digital evidence: A guide for law enforcement*. http://nij.gov/nij/pubs-sum/199408.htm.

NIJ (2008). Electronic crime scene investigation: A guide for first responders, Second Edition. http://www.nij.gov/pubs-sum/219941.htm.

Quick, D., & Choo, K.-K. R. (2016). Big forensic data reduction: digital forensic images and electronic evidence. *Cluster Computing, 19*(2), 723–740.

Ratcliffe, J. (2008). Intelligence-led policing. *Trends and Issues in Crime and Criminal Justice*. Australian Institute of Criminology.

Rogers, M. (2003). The role of criminal profiling in the computer forensics process. *Computers and Security, 22*(4), 292–298.

Toddington_International (2016). *Online investigator's checklist*, Toddington International Inc. Retrieved July 7, 2016, from https://1x7meb3bmahktmrx39tuiync-wpengine.netdna-ssl.com/wp-content/uploads/TII_Online-Investigators-Checklist_v2-1.pdf.

UNODC. (2011). *United nations office on drugs and crime—Criminal intelligence manual for analysts*. New York, Vienna, Austria: United Nations.

Weiser, M., Biros, D. P., & Mosier, G. (2006). Development of a national repository of digital forensic intelligence. In *Proceedings of the conference on digital forensics, security and law*.

Chapter 6
Summary

In this Volume, the process of Quick Analysis was outlined, with examples using test data and real world data used to explain the process in detail, and provide an overview of its real world application. The use of digital forensic data for intelligence analysis and the benefits of digital forensic data for intelligence led policing was then explored, highlighting the importance of cross-case and cross-device analysis, leading to a process to examine mobile device extracts, and reduce the volume of the data for analysis purposes. The fusion of digital forensic data with open source and closed source data was then explored, using test data, and the process explained in terms of real world data.

The overall theme of this research is examination of the digital forensic data volume issue affecting digital forensic analysis demands, and to research and propose valid methods to address the increasing volume of devices and data with methodologies encompassed in a framework which is applicable to real world investigation demands.

In Volume 1, a Framework to encompass Digital Forensic Data Reduction and Data Mining was outlined (reproduced in this Volume in Fig. 1.1), and each of the stages were outlined, then covered in depth in Volumes 1 and 2.

The processes and methods were designed using the test data corpus and applied to real world data to ensure applicability with the real world observed number of devices and data volume. The implications of the research relate to providing a method for digital forensic practitioners to process increasing numbers of devices with increasing volumes of data, and an ability to collect and process relevant evidence and intelligence in a timely manner. The Framework also provides a capability to switch to full forensic imaging and analysis should the need arise, and is encouraged should the rapid collection and analysis process not locate evidence or intelligence.

Other digital forensic frameworks for digital forensics, such as those of ACPO (2006); McKemmish (1999); NIJ (2004, 2008) focus on evidential analysis of full forensic images, whereas the Framework outlined in this research includes a process of rapid review where appropriate. An advantage of this is that practitioners can control the speed of an investigation, and if evidence or intelligence is rapidly located, they can move on to the next investigation in a timely manner, which benefits practitioners in an organisation, investigators, victims and suspects (with a timely result), legal and Court staff, and society in general.

D. Quick and K.-K. R. Choo, *Big Digital Forensic Data*, SpringerBriefs on Cyber Security Systems and Networks, https://doi.org/10.1007/978-981-13-0263-3_6

Digital Forensic Data Reduction by Selective Imaging (DRbSI) (outlined in Volume 1) encompasses a method to reduce the volume of data, as called for by other researchers (Beebe and Clark 2005; Palmer 2001) and has demonstrated a capability to reduce the original source media to 0.206% of the volume, and still retain key evidence and intelligence information. The data subsets are then used in the Quick Analysis process (Fig. 2.1) which guides the process of digital forensic analysis. In research this was explored using DRbSI data subsets and full forensic images inclusive of test data and then applied to real-world data. The method provides a manner for practitioners to undertake a rapid review of a subset of data, or apply the method to full forensic images and addresses the need to outline a process of thorough analysis. Current analysis methodologies, such as; 'Putting it all together' (Bunting 2012), the US DoJ Digital Forensic Analysis Methodology (Carroll et al. 2007, 2008), and/or the US NIJ Analysis Guidelines (NIJ 2004), focus on specific tools or investigation typologies. As outlined in Chap. 2, the proposed Quick Analysis methodology addresses a need for a method of analysis which encompasses a range of tools, and can be applied to a range of investigations.

Following this, a method to semi-automate a process of data fusion of digital forensic DRbSI data subsets with external source data in an effort to expand the knowledge and value of the information and data holdings. The process detailed in Fig. 5.1, as applied to test data, highlighted the ability to semi-automate a process of value-adding to the data holdings within a data subset with the inclusion of external source data, in this case open source data. The process of reviewing external source data also includes the ability to include closed source data holdings, such as; internal records of a government agency, and confidential source data, such as; surveillance information or other classified information. The DFINT+OSINT process has potential to contribute to a knowledge base of digital forensic data, such as that proposed by Weiser et al. (2006), and expand on the opportunity to locate disparate cross-case linkages. When undertaken in a timely manner, this can assist with appropriate resourcing of investigations, with a potential for a timely resolution of investigations.

With these processes encompassed within the framework a solution is achieved to the digital forensic data volume issue which provides practitioners with the tools necessary to process digital forensic data in a timely manner.

6.1 Conclusion

In Volume 1 it was concluded that the number of devices and the volume of data associated with digital forensic analysis has increased dramatically over recent years. This has led to increasing backlogs of work in many digital forensic labs across the globe, and has been described as the "greatest single challenge." In the review of published literature, a variety of proposed solutions were explored, yet none were located that were able to be successfully applied to reduce a volume of electronic evidence. The conclusion of the literature review was that of the many proposed solutions, data reduction had potential to impact across the entire process of digital forensic analysis, which was then shown to be the case.

The framework to guide the process of data reduction and rapid analysis was then outlined (reproduced in Fig. 1.1; Digital Forensic Data Reduction Framework) and tested to ensure it provides for a method to guide the process of data reduction and timely analysis. Next, the process of data reduction was developed to include semi-automated selection of key data and files, which are preserved in a digital forensic logical container, providing for current and future analysis needs.

A process of rapid review enables practitioners to undertake advanced analysis of the data subsets in a timely manner, with a thorough process designed to locate evidence and intelligence from a wide range of files and data holdings. This process is also applicable to a wide range of devices and data extracts, including computers, hard drives, storage media, mobile phones, portable devices, Internet-of-Things (IoT) devices, and embedded systems.

A process of cross-device and cross-case analysis enables data points from a range of cases to be located and assist to locate evidence and intelligence across a wide range of suspected offending. The inclusion of external source data, such as is available from closed source, confidential source, and importantly, from open source data holdings, serves to greatly improve the value of the data holdings.

The process of Digital Forensic Quick Analysis provides practitioners with a process to undertake rapid analysis of data subsets whilst maintaining the need for a thorough review of the data, and this is also applicable to full forensic image analysis, providing for a guiding framework to ensure evidence and intelligence is discovered in a timely manner.

The process of Digital Forensic Intelligence expands individual data point analysis to include a range of devices observed within common investigations, and also expands this to include disparate case analysis which may lead to uncovering cross-case linkages previously unknown. The process of Digital Forensic Intelligence plus Open Source Intelligence (DFINT+OSINT) provides a mechanism to gather external source data relevant to digital forensic data holdings, and greatly improve the value of the data.

The Digital Forensic Quick Analysis methodology guides the process of digital forensic analysis to undertake a rapid review of a subset of data, or full forensic image analysis, and addresses a need for a method of analysis which encompasses a range of tools, and can be applied to a range of investigations.

The fusion of digital forensic DRbSI data subsets with external source data provides a capability to expand the knowledge and value of digital forensic information and data holdings. The DFINT+OSINT process has potential to contribute to a knowledge base of digital forensic data with the opportunity to locate disparate cross-case linkages. When undertaken in a timely manner, this can assist with appropriate resourcing of investigations, with a potential for a timely resolution of investigations.

References

All URLs were last accessed (and correct) on 5 November 2016

ACPO (2006). *Good practice guidelines for computer based evidence v4.0*, Association of Chief Police Officers. Retrieved March 5, 2014, from www.7safe.com/electronic_evidence.

Beebe, N., & Clark, J. (2005). Dealing with terabyte data sets in digital investigations. *Advances in Digital Forensics*, 3–16.

Bunting, S. (2012). *EnCase computer forensics—The official EnCE EnCase certified examiner study guide* (3rd ed.). Chichester: Wiley.

Carroll, O., Brannon, S., & Song, T. (2007). *Digital forensic analysis methodology*. Retrieved September 19, 2007, from www.cybercrime.gov/forensics_gov/forensicschart.pdf.

Carroll, O., Brannon, S., & Song, T. (2008). Computer forensics: Digital forensic analysis methodology. *United States Attorneys' Bulletin: Computer Forensics, 56*(1), 65.

McKemmish, R. (1999). *What is forensic computing?*

NIJ (2004). *Forensic examination of digital evidence: A guide for law enforcement*. http://nij.gov/nij/pubs-sum/199408.htm.

NIJ (2008). *Electronic crime scene investigation: A guide for first responders* (2nd ed). http://www.nij.gov/pubs-sum/219941.htm.

Palmer, G. (2001). A road map for digital forensic research. In *Report from the first digital forensic research workshop (DFRWS)*, August 7–8, 2001.

Weiser, M., Biros, D. P., & Mosier, G. (2006). Development of a national repository of digital forensic intelligence. In *Proceedings of the conference on digital forensics, security and law*.

Printed in the United States
By Bookmasters